APOLOGIE DE LA DANSE

APOLOGIE DE LA DANSE

by F. De Lauze 1623

A Treatise of Instruction in

DANCING AND DEPORTMENT

given in the Original French
with a Translation, Introduction
and Notes by
JOAN WILDEBLOOD

Music transcribed by
EDUARDO M. TORNER

Noverre Press

First published in 1952

This facsimile reprint published in 2010 by
The Noverre Press
Southwold House
Isington Road
Binsted
Hampshire
GU34 4PH

ISBN 978-1-906830-10-6

A CIP catalogue record for this book is available from the British Library

CONTENTS

Translator's Note	11
Introduction	13
Aux Cavaliers et aux Dames par Luy Mesme	34
Dedication to My Lord Marquess of Buckingham	37
Notice	43
Preface	49
An Apology for the Dance	59
The Method for Gentlemen	83
On the Principles of the Dance	85
On the Bow	85
On the *Courante* in General	87
On the *Courante*	89
On the Bow before beginning the *Courante*	91
On the *Courante Reglée*	93
On the more Necessary Actions which should be observed in the *Courante*	95
On the *Bransles*	99
On the Bow before beginning the *Bransles*	101
On the First *Bransle*	103
On the Second *Bransle*	105
On the Third *Bransle*	105
On the *Gaillarde*	111
On the *Capriole*	115
On the Bow in order to salute a Lord or a Lady	121

CONTENTS

Dedication to My Lady Marchioness of Buckingham	127
The Method for Ladies	129
On Principles	131
On the Curtsy	131
On the First *Bransle*	135
On the *Bransle Gay*	137
On the *Bransle de Poitou*	139
On the Fourth *Bransle*	141
On the Fifth *Bransle*	143
On the *Gavotte*	145
On the *Courante*	145
On the *Gaillarde*	149

Simplified instructions, with notes and comparisons with contemporary documents for:

(*a*) Deportment	162
(*b*) Dancing	176

(*a*) DEPORTMENT

The ordinary Bow used when Greeting an Acquaintance	162
The Bow before the *Courante*	163
The Bow before the *Bransles*	165
The Bow to Salute a Lord	166
The Bow to Salute a Lady	167
The Procedure to be observed when asking a Lady to dance	171
The Lady's Curtsy	173
The Lady's Passing Curtsy	174

CONTENTS

(b) DANCING

The *Capriole, Demi-capriole,* and *Entrechat*	176
Pas Coupé	179
Entre-coupé	181
Pas Assemblé	181
Pas Chassé	182
Pas Couler	183
Pas Glissé	184
Glissade	184
The *Fleuret*	184
Retirade	185
The *Gaillarde*	185
The *Courante*	191
The *Bransles*	192
The First *Bransle*	198
The Second *Bransle*	202
The Third *Bransle*	203
The Fourth *Bransle*	210
The Fifth *Bransle*	212
The *Gavotte*	216
Music from *Harmonie Universelle*	155–161
Bibliography of Books referred to in the Introduction and Notes	218
Index	219

ILLUSTRATIONS

George Villiers, First Duke of Buckingham (1590–1628), with his Wife and Two Children *facing page* 16
(Reproduced by gracious permission of H.M. the King. Photo: A. C. Cooper, F.R.P.S.)

A Ball 17

Two Examples of Poise 32
(Reproduced by permission of Lord De L'Isle and Dudley, V.C.)

A Nobleman leading a Bransle 33

A Dancing Party 33

Ceremony of signing a Marriage Contract in the King's Bedchamber 176

A Marriage Feast 176

A Young Knight kissing his Hand as he receives the Accolade from Louis XIII 177

French Nobility 177

A Nobleman of Lorraine bowing 192

Lady snapping her Fingers in Dancing 192

A Bow in the Italian Style 193

Dedicated
to the Memory of
MARK EDWARD PERUGINI
in grateful remembrance of his
kindness and interest

•

NOTE

ANY specialised subject has a language of its own, and the art of dancing is no exception. The difficulty of elucidating these early dance terms is well recognised. Some terms used by De Lauze bear the same meaning today, as, to take one example, the expression "with the feet closed", which any modern ballet dancer will understand, though the layman might not do so. Therefore, as this book is not intended for dancers only, the English translation here reads "with the feet together", for the purpose of the translation has been to attempt to make the instructions as clear as possible to the modern reader. The somewhat obscure style of the original renders the exact interpretation of certain passages difficult, even to expert linguists whom I have consulted. The value, therefore, of this publication lies partly in the fact that this rare work is here reproduced in the original French, thanks to the enterprise and artistry of the publishers.

To Lucile Armstrong, whose knowledge both of the French language and of dancing gave me invaluable assistance in the English translation, I wish to express my deepest gratitude. Also to John Palmer for his advice on many points in connection with the translation. Professor Torner's knowledge of ancient dance music and dance rhythms enabled me to work with greater confidence on the dances, thereby enhancing the value of the original work by De Lauze by the inclusion of contemporary music for the *Suite of Bransles*. Although the *Bransle* has been treated of in general before now, there is to my knowledge no work which has dealt with this important *suite* in a similar manner.

In past ages the art of good manners was incorporated

NOTE

into the art of dancing, even as it still survives in the traditional courtly dances of the West and the East. Although this is common knowledge, it is less common to find authentic and detailed descriptions of how such courtesies as *bowing, curtsying, greeting an acquaintance*, and so forth were performed. This work of De Lauze is thus of great interest, not only to anyone connected with the theatre, but to those who find entertainment in former modes of life and behaviour. Comparisons with other contemporary sources of information have been introduced merely in order to explain certain fashions in deportment mentioned by De Lauze which otherwise might not be understood.

I am grateful to Mr. C. W. Beaumont for allowing me to use his translations of Arbeau and Rameau in my quotations from these works. I also wish to express my thanks to the authors and publishers for permission to quote from *George Villiers, 1st Duke of Buckingham*, by Hugh Ross Williamson (Duckworth), *Modes and Manners*, by Max von Boëhn (Harrap), *The Witch-cult in Western Europe*, by Margaret Alice Murray (Clarendon Press), and *England as seen by Foreigners in the days of Elizabeth and James I*, by William Brenchley Rye (J. R. Smith).

I would also like to acknowledge the courteous assistance of the Staff of the Reading Room, British Museum.

J. W.

London, 1950.

INTRODUCTION

ALTHOUGH prior to the nineteenth century dancing was considered an essential feature of any gentleman's, or gentlewoman's, education, it is only in recent years that this art has struggled to regain its status as a recognised element of culture.

The interest evoked by the Ballet has led to an unprecedented demand for literature on the subject. There are a number of excellent books on the history of the dance in general, while others have shown the importance of this medium of expression in the lives of primitive tribes. On the other hand, there is, in England at least, a lack of authentic information regarding the manner in which our ancestors danced. This information is in fact available, but it is not easily accessible, for the records which divulge this knowledge were once regarded as being of mere transitory value. The majority were either lost or damaged, so that today they are exceedingly rare.

Dance movement is well reputed to be one of the most difficult things to write down. However good the method of writing or notating these movements may be, it is never completely satisfactory, the only sure way being to transmit it, so to speak, from foot to foot. There is, however, one disadvantage with this method. It would be unnatural if dancing did not develop and change throughout the years. As this change takes place, the old method is naturally forgotten. It is therefore not safe to assume that because a "tradition" has been retained of certain dances or movements, these are necessarily the same as the originals. It is necessary to examine the source of the "tradition", as, for instance, that of the stage *Minuet* of today.

INTRODUCTION

The original *Minuet*, which, it is believed, developed from a *Bransle* of the seventeenth century, probably owed its popularity to the fact that, both in steps and pattern, it was more simple than many of the "figured" French dances then in vogue. "The *Menuet* has become the most fashionable dance, due to the felicity with which it may be performed, and to the easy figure now in use" (Rameau).

It is evident that throughout the eighteenth century the dance underwent some superficial changes, for even in Rameau's time certain "embellishments" were being introduced by way of variety, and figured *Minuets* were coming into fashion, but up to the end of the eighteenth century the true *Minuet* retained its characteristic pattern and steps.

Even when dancing-masters composed a solo *Minuet*, or *Minuets* for groups of young ladies, or for couples in the form of a Country Dance, the basic step was the same *Minuet* step, and the figure of the dance nearly always included at least a suggestion of the characteristic "S" figure.

The simple, basic steps used in stage dances of the eighteenth century were identically the same as those used in the ballroom. The difference lay in the manner of presenting these steps: for example, John Weaver wrote: "as *Common-Dancing*" [ballroom-dancing] "has a peculiar Softness, which would hardly be perceivable on the Stage; so *Stage-Dancing* would have a rough and ridiculous Air in a Room."

Also the more intricate steps, such as beats and high springs, were regarded as suitable for the stage but not for the ballroom.

In the nineteenth century this state of things changed considerably. The ballroom dances of this period had not the same theatrical value as those of earlier periods. Moreover, references to such dances as the *Gaillarde*, *Courante*, and

INTRODUCTION

Minuet occur in the older plays, and as these were no longer in fashion, it became necessary to "revive" (or invent) them.

The *Minuets* composed by the dancing-masters of the nineteenth century were, both in steps and character, entirely unlike the true *Minuets* of the eighteenth century. Such masters did not conceal the fact that they considered their inventions to be more "graceful" and "genteel" than the original dance. Of such is the *Minuet* which has become the tradition of the stage. It has its place in the history of stage dancing, but if accuracy from an historical or educational point of view is desired, one must look farther into the past. Latterly there has arisen a wish for greater authenticity in period costume on the stage, and this should also apply to the dancing. Costume and dance are so closely interdependent that the mere donning of an authentic dress cannot make unauthentic steps and dances appear convincing.

A debt of gratitude is due to Mr. C. W. Beaumont for his translation and republication of two important dance treatises: *Orchésographie*, by Thoinot Arbeau (Langres, 1588), and *Le Maître à danser*, by P. Rameau (Paris, 1725). Mr. Beaumont truly says of the *Orchésographie* that it "is a detailed treatise on the society dances in vogue throughout the sixteenth century", and of *Le Maître à danser* that it is "the standard work on the technique of eighteenth-century dancing".

It is usually difficult to discover much about the lives of early dancing-masters or those who wrote on dancing. Occasionally the former gained prestige through becoming members of some lord's household, but apart from this they were seldom men of particular renown. De Lauze may, or may not, have become a dancing-master by profession. One cannot assume that he was from the fact that he wrote a treatise on dancing.

INTRODUCTION

Thoinot Arbeau and Marin Mersenne were among those about whom we know something, but they were not merely recorders of the art of dancing!

Thoinot Arbeau was the pen-name assumed by Jehan Tabourot, a priest, born at Dijon in 1519, who became Canon of Langres, where he died in 1595. Previous to his *Orchésographie* he had published a book on astronomy.

Father Mersenne, theologian, mathematician, and philosopher, was born in the hamlet of La Soultière (Maine) in 1588. He studied at the college of La Flêche, where Descartes followed him a few years later. Mersenne wrote some important treatises on music, his most valuable work being *Harmonie Universelle*, published in 1636. He died in Paris in 1648, as the result of an operation.

It is possible that De Lauze may have lived, or at least spent some time, at Blois. This is merely a speculation based on the following scraps of information: (*a*) Blois was a resort of the Court of Louis XIII; (*b*) it was noted as a stronghold of the Calvinists—it was obviously against the views held by such persons that De Lauze dictated his *Apologie de la Danse*; (*c*) according to Williamson, it is known that George Villiers spent a considerable portion of his stay in France at Blois; (*d*) Arbeau, whom De Lauze mentions as a friend, obtained the King's Privilege for his *Orchésographie* at Blois.

De Lauze's reference to Arbeau's *Orchésographie* seems to show that the former consulted Arbeau before writing his *Apologie de la Danse*.

It may be that De Lauze began his book some years before it was published. In any case, the *Apologie de la Danse* bridges the gap between the two well-known treatises of Arbeau and Rameau.

As an exponent of his subject, De Lauze does not compare favourably with either of the above. He fully lives up to the general affectation of the writers of his time, whose am-

GEORGE VILLIERS, FIRST DUKE OF BUCKINGHAM (1590–1628), WITH HIS WIFE AND TWO CHILDREN

(From the painting by Gerard Honthorst (1590-1656). Reproduced by gracious permission of His Majesty the King)

A BALL
(Note gentleman in background kissing his hand to a lady)

INTRODUCTION

biguous and flowery language often all but obliterates their meaning.

Nevertheless, his book is worth reading for several reasons.

In an age when the manners of the Court were becoming increasingly artificial, the observance of the correct mode of behaviour became a matter of supreme importance, especially for those members of society who desired to appear to advantage in courtly circles.

This "science of behaviour towards others", says De Lauze (*entregent* is the apt word used), "is necessary to youth . . .". He therefore lays down the exact method of saluting a lord or lady, and the precise procedure that was needful in asking a lady to dance. This appears to be the earliest detailed information to be published today on how the bows and curtsies of this period were performed.

The seventeenth century was a period which had a far-reaching influence on the future art of dancing, particularly of Ballet, in Europe. The Court Masques, which had been a popular form of entertainment for many years, now reached a state of extravagant elaboration so far unsurpassed. "Theatricals were a form of entertainment which naturally found favour in all places and among all classes. . . . For courts, bound as they were by the rules of an iron etiquette, if human relations were to be maintained between ruler and subjects, theatricals were a real necessity. A kind of mummery, called *Wirtschaft*, was therefore devised at which, for the duration of the festival, the ruling prince and princesses took the parts of host and hostesses, the court those of serving-men and maids, house-boys, and so on. Germans were particularly fond of this kind of diversion, and frequent mention of such *Wirtschaften* occurs in the letters of Sophia, Electress of Hanover, for they provided a very useful means of solving the endless difficulties created by points of etiquette when guests of note had to

INTRODUCTION

be entertained...." (From *Modes and Manners*, by Max von Boëhn, translated by Joan Joshua, Vol. III, *The Seventeenth Century*.)

Masques of this nature were performed at the marriages of important persons and on any occasion of note. An important item of these Court festivals was the dancing.

In the spectacular Ballets (the Ballet being then a combination of song, dance, and spoken dialogue), the dancing was performed by the members of the Court. That the proficiency of this aristocratic *corps de ballet* did not always satisfy the high ideals of the Sun King, Louis XIV of France, is suggested by letters written at the inauguration of the *Académie Royale de la Danse*, which was set up in Paris in the year 1661. It seems that one purpose of this body was to maintain a high standard of dancing for these semi-political functions, which were designed partly to impress distinguished visitors from other Courts. It was the members of this Academy who, by degrees, devised the rules and precepts which laid the foundation of modern Ballet. The dancing on which they based their technique was that which De Lauze describes.

He is most insistent throughout on the "turn out" of the legs and feet, a convention which forms the basis of Ballet technique. That this convention was only beginning to be practised is seen from his remark that "many masters consider it is not necessary to oblige a *lady* to point her toes outwards, and they found this opinion on the fact that, as they are not seen, it does not matter what action they have". He, however, concludes his argument with a plea for the necessity of this practice.

Another point of interest is the suggestion, made by De Lauze, that the novice should practise the correct movements of the legs while holding on to a table for support. Though it is not claimed that De Lauze originated this idea, we find here the theory which in time became

INTRODUCTION

formulated into the practice of *exercises à la barre*, which is the backbone of technical training in Ballet.

One feels regret that his instructions are not more explicit. He may possibly be excused on the grounds of his own admission, that this treatise was but an essay which, if well received and sponsored by so eminent a personage as George Villiers, 1st Duke of Buckingham, would give him sufficient encouragement to produce a greater and, one fears, an even more wordy effort.

In the days when most authors sought the patronage of some distinguished member of society, it is not surprising that anyone who wished to procure an English *clientèle* should choose the man who, at that time, held a position of supreme favour at the English Court. The adulatory epistles dedicated to such personages were of a more or less uniform character, but in this instance the tribute was not wholly misplaced.

George Villiers was a man who possessed great charm of manner and good looks. His widowed mother encouraged those traits in her son, which augured well for a career at Court. So this lad, "finding Nature more indulgent to him in the ornaments of the body than of the mind, the tendency of his youthful genius was rather to improve those excellencies wherein his choice felicity consisted, than to addict himself to morose and sullen bookishness; therefore his chief exercises were dancing, fencing, vaulting, etc." (From *George Villiers, 1st Duke of Buckingham*, by H. R. Williamson.)

After a stay in France to finish his studies, Villiers returned to England in 1613, "with the distinction of being the finest dancer in the country" (Williamson). He soon became the particular favourite of King James I, and quickly ascended to the highest ranks of the nobility. In 1616 he became Master of the Horse, was created Viscount Villiers and Knight of the Garter. In 1617 he was created

INTRODUCTION

Earl, and in 1618 Marquess, the title by which De Lauze addresses him, for James only conferred the dukedom upon him in May 1623, while Villiers was abroad with Prince Charles.

Katherine Villiers, Duchess of Buckingham, to whom De Lauze dedicates his *Method for Ladies*, was Lady Katherine Manners, daughter of the Earl of Rutland. James, who doted on Buckingham, was godfather to their first child, Mary, who was born in March 1622. "Little Mall", as she was called, apparently inherited her father's love of dancing, if one can believe a mother's biased opinion.

In the summer of 1623, Katherine wrote to her husband: "My Lord, indeed I must crave your pardon that I did write you no more particulars of our pretty Mall. I did tell dry-nurse what you write to me, and she says you had one letter from her, and she has sent you word by everyone that has gone, that she was well, and what she could do; but if you will pardon me this fault, I will commit the like no more. She is very well, I thank God, and when she is set to her feet, and held by her sleeves" [these were the long strings which fell down the back from the shoulders which are often seen in portraits of these times] "she will not go softly, but stamp and set one foot afore another very fast, that I think she will run before she can go. She loves dancing extremely, and when the Sarabande is played, she will set her thumb and her finger together, offering to snap; and then when *Tom Duff* is sunge, then she will shake her apron; and when she hears the tune of the clapping dance my Lady Frances Huberd taught the Prince, she will clap both her hands together and on her breast, and she can tell the tunes as well as any of us can; and as they change the tunes, she will change her dancing. I would you were here but to see her, for you would take much delight in her now she is so full of pretty play and tricks; and she has gotten a trick that when they dance her, she will cry 'Hah! Hah!',

INTRODUCTION

and Nicholas" [Edward Nicholas, secretary to Buckingham] "will dance with his legs, and she will imitate him as well as she can. She will be excellent at a Hat, for if one lay her down, she will kick her legs over her head, but when she is older, I hope she will be more modest. Everybody says she grows every day more like you. You shall have her picture very shortly." (*Harl. MSS.*, British Museum.)

Buckingham was at this time in Spain with Prince Charles (later Charles I), with the object of settling the negotiations for the proposed marriage of Charles to the Infanta Maria. This knight-errant visit of Charles to Spain had been conceived by Buckingham, and the two of them had set out on their journey in February 1623—"disguised in false beards, under the names of John and Thomas Smith" (Williamson). The disguise was to prevent the English from discovering that their Prince was risking his person in placing himself at the mercy of a foreign power. The marriage negotiations broke down, and it seems that Buckingham's behaviour in Spain had not improved matters.

If as a Minister of State Buckingham was a disaster, as an ornament of the Court he excelled. Williamson says that King James I "in spite of his chronic poverty . . . gave £1,500 towards the preparation of a new Masque, of which dancing was to be the principal feature 'for the gracing of young Villiers, and to bring him on the stage' ".

If De Lauze had wished to set up a school of dance instruction in England, he could have had no better introduction.

French dancing-masters were by no means rare in England during the seventeenth century. They were a recognised butt for the satirist.

The famous Jacques Cordier (known as Bocan) was employed in England about 1610–11 for the production of Court masques. He taught the queens of Spain, Poland,

INTRODUCTION

and Denmark, and in 1622 was dancing-master to Henrietta Maria.

It seems that, although Bocan was unable to read or to note music, his gift for playing the violin made him famous, not only in his own time, for his influence on French instrumental music is considered to have been not insignificant. The *Bocane*, which was a figured *Courante*, is supposed to have been named after him.

A knowledge of music and dancing was an integral part of any gentleman's education. Those who had imbibed this knowledge in their upbringing had an advantage over others who had possibly been less fortunate.

It is evident that Samuel Pepys and his "poor wife" came under the category of these less fortunate members of society.

Their obvious desire to become proficient in what was then considered an important social grace is revealed by the following entries in *Pepys's Diary*:

"*April* 19*th* (1663).—After supper fell in discourse of dancing, and I find Ashwell hath a very fine carriage, which makes my wife almost ashamed of herself to see herself so outdone, but tomorrow she begins to learn to dance for a month or two.

"*May* 4*th*.—The dancing-master come, whom standing by, seeing him instructing my wife, when he had done with her, he would needs have me try the steps of a *coranto*: and what with his desire and my wife's importunity, I did begin, and then was obliged to give him entry money 10*s*. and am become his scholar. The truth is, I think it is a thing very useful for any gentleman.

"*May* 8*th*.—At supper comes Pembleton, and afterwards we all up to dancing till late. They say that I am like to make a dancer.

"*May* 12*th*.—A little angry with my wife for minding

INTRODUCTION

nothing now but the dancing-master, having him come twice a day, which is folly.

"*May* 16*th.*—After dinner comes Pembleton again, and I did go up to them to practise, and did make an end of *La Duchesse*" [this was presumably a "figured" *Courante* which bore this name], "which I think I should, with a little pains, do very well."

In spite of all this trouble, however, Pepys's nerve apparently failed him at the thought of dancing before the "Quality". After dining with George Waterman, Sheriff of London, two years later, he records: "Very good cheer we had, and merry music at and after dinner, and a fellow danced a jigg; but when the company began to dance, I come away, *lest I should be taken out*; and God knows how my wife carried herself, but I left her to try her fortune."

This remark did not refer, as might appear to the uninitiated, to the probability of Pepys being in an inebriated condition, but to his fear of being asked to dance, or "taken out" by some lady. It does suggest, at the same time, that the standard of dancing was tolerably high.

It is worth quoting Antoine de Courtin, even at some length, for the illuminating picture he draws of the manners of the ballroom in his time:

"If [a man] knows how to Dance, it is not handsome to be difficult; but if his talent be but indifferent, he must not pretend to over-much skill, nor engage himself in Dances he does not understand, at least but imperfectly.

"If his ear be not good, he is, if possible, to decline it, though he knows his steps never so well; for what can be more ridiculous than to see a man out in his time, and the whole company in confusion by his means; for he might have excused himself, and he pleased, by leading the Lady into the middle of the Hall, and making a low *Congy*" [i.e.

a bow]. "But he ought first to signify the displeasure he conceived in not being skilled in that excellent Recreation, that she might be satisfied it was not Contempt, or Morosity, so much as want of address.

"But if after all our Apologies they—for their divertisement—will oblige us to Dance, we must by no means refuse; for 'tis much better to expose ourselves to some little involuntary disorder in being complaisant, than be suspected of pride. In that case we must with as good language as we are able, intreat the Lady that she would vouchsafe to Dance some Dance we conceive we understand, which we must Dance afterwards frankly, and as well as we can.

"Having finisht our Dance, we are to attend that Lady to her place, and with a low reverence take out another: observing when we are taken out again, to return our revenge upon the Lady which took us out first, if it be the custom of that place" [this was in the sense of returning a compliment], "and by no means to possess ourselves of the seat which belongs to any one that is Dancing."

With regard to the etiquette of returning the compliment Rameau gives the same advice: "But if you are asked to dance again, you must, when it is your turn to invite a lady, choose the one who asked you in the first place, otherwise you would commit a grave breach of good manners. This rule applies equally to ladies."

It was usual for the man to conduct the lady back to her place after dancing. If, however, the King or Queen were present at the ball, it seems that it was not permissible to fetch out, or conduct, the ladies to and from their seats. According to *The Rules of Civility* (1685), "if the King or Queen be at a Ball, you are not to take the Ladies out, nor return them to their places; but you are, with a low *Congy*, to invite them, and when you have done, having paid them the same reverence, you may let them pass alone to their seats".

INTRODUCTION

In order to comply with the regulated order of the ball, it was necessary to perform the ceremonious bows and curtsies, even if the dancer who had been "taken out" thereupon excused himself, or herself, on the grounds that he, or she, could not dance. As this must have appeared both foolish and tiresome, it is hardly surprising that those, who felt dubious of their skill in this accomplishment, should prefer to stay away from a ball, rather than risk "a little involuntary disorder".

The *Apologie de la Danse* is not a specification of all the dances which were in fashion at this time, for De Lauze only wished to describe those which, in his opinion, were "the most advantageous".

The dances mentioned by Mersenne as being danced in France are *Passemezzes*, *Pavanes*, *Allemands*, *Sarabandes*, *Voltes*, *Courantes*, *Canaries*, *Bransles*, and *Ballets*. Of these he says the *Courante* was the dance most generally in use, and was danced by one couple at a time.

The Courante.—Rameau writes that "formerly the teaching of dancing began with the *Courante*", although at the time of writing his book (1725), the fashion for this dance had faded, to be supplanted by the *Minuet*.

De Lauze is therefore in accord with the practice of his times in beginning with a discourse upon the *Courante*.

During the seventeenth century, the *Courante* developed into what Rameau styles a very noble dance, composed of many steps and figures. The sixteenth-century *Courante*, given in Arbeau's *Orchésographie*, in which the damsels flung themselves into their partner's arms and danced "pell-mell", belonged to the bad old days, when, in De Lauze's opinion, people danced anyhow.

The slow *Courante* of the later seventeenth century was a stately dance, of gliding movements danced in 3/2 time, by only one couple at a time. These *danses à deux* usually followed the *Bransles*, and were, so to speak, the high light

INTRODUCTION

of the entertainment. The *Courante* held this place of honour in the heyday of the dancing years of Louis XIV.

Charles II of England had had plenty of opportunity to practise this noble art during the years of his exile in France, and was reputed to be a fine dancer. At the ball at Whitehall where Pepys watched the dancing with Mr. Povey, he says: "After that" [i.e. the *bransle*] "the King led a lady a single *Courante*, and then the rest of the lords, one after the other: very noble it was and great pleasure to see. . . . The manner was, when the King dances, all the ladies in the room, and the Queen herself, stand up" [i.e. *as well as* the men]. "And indeed he dances finely, and much better than the Duke of York."

The Bransles.—The circle, or round-dance, in which the dancers form either a complete, or partial, circle, is generally recognised to be one of the oldest forms of the group dance. It is natural that this should be so, for it is a pattern into which a mass of people will easily form if they are either dancing round some object, as in worship, or, if being joined one to another by holding hands, linking arms, or placing their arms across each other's shoulders, or backs, their dance continues to *progress*, either forwards, backwards, or sideways, without leaving the same dancing ground.

Another ancient form of *group dancing* is the "processional" or "follow-my-leader" type, where the dancers fall in, either singly or in pairs, behind a leader, whom they are obliged to follow wherever he chooses to lead them. These two formations were often combined, for the *processional* dance might start some distance away from the dancing ground, and possibly finish as a *round-dance* when the chosen spot had been reached.

The winding about of the *processional* dance, and the final circle of the *round-dance*, is picturesquely described in the well-known poem by Sir John Davies (1596).

INTRODUCTION

How Love taught them to Dance

Then first of all he doth demonstrate plaine
The motions seven that are in nature found,
Upward and downward, forth and back again,
To this side and to that, and turning round;
Whereof a thousand Brawles *he doth compound*
Which he doth teach unto the multitude,
And ever with a turne they must conclude.

. . .

As when a nymph arysing from the Lande,
Leadeth a daunce with her long watery traine
Down to the sea, she wries to every hand,
And every way doth cross the fertile plaine:
But when at last she falls into the maine,
Then all her traverses concluded are,
And with the Sea her course is circulaire.

In both the *processional* and the *round-dance*, it was usual to have a leader—the *ring-leader*—who led the pattern, set the pace, and whose actions had to be followed, and either imitated or responded to by the company. This leader was often the one who sang the verses of the song, while the rest of the company replied in the chorus, a feature of many folk-dances to this day.

The dance-hymn was one of the earliest forms of ritual worship, not only in the pre-Christian era, for it was not abandoned with many other pagan rites, but was incorporated in the ceremonies of the early Christian Church.

The mediæval French *carole* was modelled on this ancient song-dance of worship. The *carole*, which was a chain-dance in either a closed or open ring, was danced, as a rule, to the accompaniment of song, though instruments are also known to have been used.

INTRODUCTION

Although it is customary to associate these *caroles*, which, it seems, became known later in the fifteenth century as *Bransles*, with a string of dancers holding hands, some French dance songs of the ninth to the twelfth centuries suggest that the dancers sometimes used their arms, as in mimed gestures. We know that they did so in the sixteenth-century *Bransles*, for Arbeau describes the clapping of hands, shaking of fingers, and so forth in certain *Bransles*.

The world-wide use of this form of the dance is well known, and is too large a subject for these brief notes, but it may be of interest to record that this salient feature of pagan festivals was preserved in the clandestine rituals of the dying ancient religion in Western Europe (including Britain) for many centuries.

Dr. Margaret Murray shows this in her interesting study of the religious rites of the witches in France, Scotland, and England, gleaned from the witch trials of the seventeenth century.

Of their dances she writes: "The two principal forms of the dance were the ring-dance and the follow-my-leader dance. . . . The ring dances were usually round some object; sometimes a stone, sometimes the Devil" [who was the god of the witches] "stood or was enthroned in the middle. . . . 'Ye all danced about both the said crosses, and the meal market, a long space of time; in the which Devil's dance, thou, the said Thomas, was foremost, and led the ring, and dang the said Kathren Mitchell, because she spoiled your dance, ran not so fast about as the rest'." And again, "The round-dance was so essentially a witch dance that [Henry] More" [in his *Antidote against Atheism*, 1655] "says, 'It might be here very seasonable to enquire into the nature of those large *dark Rings* in the grass, which they call *Fairy Circles*, whether they be the *Rendezvouz* of Witches, or the dancing places of those little Puppet Spirits which they call *Elves* or *Fairies*'."

INTRODUCTION

By the fifteenth or sixteenth centuries, the round-dance had become an established feature of balls in respectable society, and was known in France as the *Bransle*, in Italy the *Brando*, and in England as *Brawls* or *Rounds*. It seems very probable that it was these *Brawls*, or *Rounds*, which were danced *round about* the Maypole during the spring, or May-day, festivities, when the youths and maidens brought back a tree from the woods, which they erected, bedecked with ribbons and garlands, as the centre of their revels.

Among the numerous accounts of these heathen merry-makings, so frowned upon by the Puritans, there does not appear to be any evidence of a Maypole dance with *ribbons* or *streamers* which the dancers *held in their hands*. On the contrary, contemporary accounts indicate that the revellers were holding on to each other!

Therefore, it seems likely that the streamer-plaiting dance of the Maypole, popularly looked upon as "an old English dance", was, in fact, an innovation of a later date.

Throughout the seventeenth century there is evidence that the ball was always commenced by dancing a *Bransle*, in England as well as in France, for at this period French fashions dominated Europe.

When Samuel Pepys went to a ball at Whitehall in 1662, he observes that the ballroom was "crammed with fine ladies, the greatest of the Court. By and by comes the King [Charles II] and the Queen, the Duke and Duchess, and all the great ones: and after seating themselves, the King takes out the Duchess of York, and the Duke the Duchess of Buckingham, the Duke of Monmouth my Lady Castlemaine, and so other lords other ladies, and they danced the *Bransle*".

In 1725 Rameau, in his *Le Maître à Danser*, asserts that the *Bransle* was still the opening dance of the ball, and that this had been the rule during the reign of Louis XIV.

We see, therefore, that the *Bransle* was one of the im-

INTRODUCTION

portant dances of the ballroom for at least 150 to 200 years. It could say of itself, "dances may come and dances may go, but I go on for ever", for while the fashion in other dances changed from the *Gaillarde* to the *Courante*, and from the *Courante* to the *Minuet*, the *Bransle* remained, though naturally it changed in steps and in manner of performance as the years went by.

It seems more than likely, too, that it may have become incorporated in the English country-dances. The garbled definition of a *Brawle*, from John Marston's play *The Malcontent* (1604), was presumably intended to convey the substance of a *Bransle* as it was then danced. It reads very like the directions for dancing some of the earlier "rounds" in Playford's *English Dancing Master* (1650):

"We have forgot the brawle."
"So soone? 'Tis wonder."
"Why? 'Tis but two singles on the left, two on the right, three doubles forward, a traverse of six round: do this twice, three singles side, galliarde trick of twentie, curranto pace: a figure of eight, three singles broken down, come up, meete, two doubles, fall backe, and then honour."
"O Dedalus! thy maze, I have quite forgot it."
"Trust me, so have I, saving the falling backe, and then honour."

The first edition, in 1650, of John Playford's famous book contains a number of round-dances, but these *rounds* gradually become fewer in the succeeding editions, till in time fashion favoured the "Longways for as many as will". In this form, each couple at the *top* retired in turn to the end of the line.

The late Cecil Sharp says of this dance: "An especial interest attaches to the Longways dances in *The Dancing Master*, for they represent the earliest examples of that type

INTRODUCTION

which, as we have seen, subsequently superseded all the others. In the seventeen editions we can trace, step by step, the gradual evolution of this type of dance, and especially of the progressive principle which eventually became its dominant feature."

Speaking of *Rounds* in country-dances, he remarks that "occasionally a progressive figure of an elementary character appears in the Round, but such occurrences are rare".

The progressive principle was a particular feature of the *Bransle de Poitou*, as is shown by De Lauze and Mersenne, and of the *Gavotte* also, as Rameau describes in his account of the King's Grand Ball: "At the conclusion of the strain, the King and Queen went to the end of the line, then the next couple led the *Bransle* in their turn, after which they took up their positions behind their Majesties. This continued until all the couples had danced and the King and Queen were at the head again. Then they danced the *Gavotte* in the same order as the *Bransle*, each couple successively retiring to the end of the line."

Now, although the *Bransle* was one of the main society dances for so many years, it is extremely difficult to find descriptions of steps that were used. Apart from Arbeau's *Orchésographie*, the only other detailed account of steps that has so far come to light is the *Apologie de la Danse* of De Lauze. Even Rameau does not trouble to write about the *Bransles*, the general attitude of these dancing-masters being that the people for whom they wrote were already sufficiently familiar with them.

The Sarabande.—"The Sarabande", says Mersenne, "was invented by the Saracens, from whence comes its name." Thus he bears out the contention that this dance was of Arabic origin, though these early writers are not always to be relied upon for their accuracy in such statements. "It is danced", he continues, "to the sound of the guitar

INTRODUCTION

and castanets—its steps are composed of *tirades* or *glissades*." The castanets, as shown in his book, are the same as are used today in Spain, and he also mentions "tous les osselets et les petits bâtons de bois, ou d'autre matière, que l'on tient entre les doigts" [all the little bones—or knuckle bones—and little sticks of wood, or other matter, which are held in the fingers].

These smaller chinking instruments were used in elegant circles in preference to the more strident castanets. It is evident that finger snapping was also used in dancing the *Sarabande*, for even a tiny child such as Mary Villiers connected the music with this practice. Even the austere Cardinal Richelieu is reputed to have danced a *Sarabande* accompanying himself with castanets.

Apart from the fact that this little treatise of De Lauze is a rare work, it is important because it shows the transition in both deportment and dance technique from that based on mediæval movements to that which heralded the modern idea.

In this the art of dancing merely reflects the pattern of life, for similar changes in architecture, language, dress, music, painting, the theatre, and so forth occurred during this period.

For this reason some comparisons have been made with the instructions given by Arbeau, Rameau, and other masters who lived during the period which immediately preceded and succeeded De Lauze.

The value of the information given in the *Apologie de la Danse* would be greater if only De Lauze had included the music, or had described the music and rhythm required. It is in the *Suite of Bransles*, with their varying changes of time and rhythm, that this lack of information is particularly unsatisfactory.

It is therefore fortunate to find not only the music, but also a brief description of these dances, by so authoritative

AN EXAMPLE OF
POISE
(*Portrait of a Boy*)

AN EXAMPLE OF
POISE
(*Princess Mary, eldest
daughter of King Charles I*)

A NOBLEMAN LEADING A BRANSLE

A DANCING PARTY

INTRODUCTION

a musician as Father Mersenne, and to discover that his account agrees so well with that of De Lauze.

It is comprehensible that there might be a slight divergence of opinion as to the exact number of steps in a *Bransle*, for it would depend largely on the writer's method of description. The technique of dancing had not yet settled into a recognised system.

> *Long was the Dancing Art unfix'd and free:*
> *Hence lost in error and Uncertainty:*
> *No Precepts did it mind, or Rules obey,*
> *But every Master taught a different Way:*

(*The Art of Dancing*, by Soame Jenyns, 1728.)

These notes have had to be too brief to do more than give an outline of the historical background, and their limitations are acknowledged.

As the history of dance steps is a subject on which comparatively little research has been attempted, it is difficult to know whether any theory presented is correct or not, and which only further discoveries can prove or disprove.

AUX CAVALIERS ET AUX DAMES PAR LUY MESME

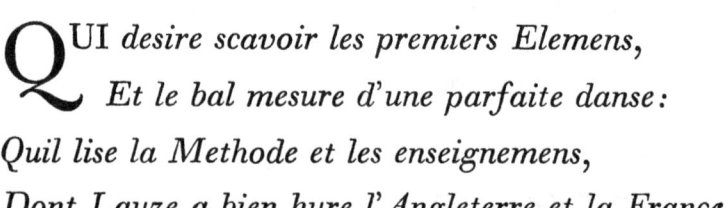

QUI *desire scavoir les premiers Elemens,*
  Et le bal mesure d'une parfaite danse:
Quil lise la Methode et les enseignemens,
Dont Lauze a bien hure l'Angleterre et la France.

Des Dames y verront parmi leurs pas divers,
L'air, l'adresse, la grace, et la grave asseurance:
Qu'elles doivent cherir. Et si les Cavaliers
Desirent aquerir la vraye cognoissance.

Soit de danser par hault, ou bien d'aler par bas,
La Lauze leur fait veior l'ordre de tous les pas,
Graves et negligens, avec temps et mesure.

Car vray Phare pour tous il a rendu parfait
Le chemin du bien estre: Joignant comme il a fait,
Et la Nature a l'art, et l'art a la Nature.

APOLOGIE DE LA DANSE

ET LA PARFAICTE METHODE
DE L'ENSEIGNER TANT AUX CAVALIERS
QUAUX DAMES

par

F. DE LAUZE
1623

A MONSEIGNEVR:

MONSEIGNEVR LE MARQVIS DE BUCKINGHAM

GRAND ESCUIER, & GRAND ADMIRAL D'ANGLETERRE, &c.

Monseignevr,

CELUY *qui offrit nagueres á vostre Grandeur comme vne nouueauté ce que i'auois Il y a quatre ans commencé sur la danse, ne m'a pas causé tant de desplaiseir de se preualoir en cela de mes peines, comme de publier vne piece qui ressentoit encores les imperfections qui accompaignent ordinairement la premiere forme qu'on donne a quelque ouurage, Car quoy qu'il s'on dise l'Autheur plusieurs auquelz la verité (de mon iuste ressentiment) n'est pas incognue, n'en pourroient veoir les impertinences sans faire quelque iugement à mon des-aduantage. Ce que voulant preuenir il ma semblé necessaire de ne plus differer a mettre en lumiere, non vne piece imparfaite ou nouuellement crayonnée, mais vn tout accompli, & que ie gardois il y a ia long temps en bon equipage de paroistre.*

Mais comme les choses (Monseignevr) *qui tiennent de l'extraordinaire ont besoing de trouuer du support dans vne authorité qui ne soit pas commune: Ce liure estant de ceste Nature (au regard de son inuention) ne pouuoit veoir le iour plus heureusement que soubz l'appuy d'un Seigneur de qui les vertus sont estimées & admiréez de tout le Monde.*

TO MY LORD MARQUESS OF BUCKINGHAM

MASTER OF THE HORSE AND GRAND ADMIRAL OF ENGLAND

MY LORD,
He who previously offered to your Excellency, as a novelty, that which I had four years since begun on the dance, did not cause me as much displeasure in his taking advantage of my work, as in publishing a piece which still carried the imperfections which usually accompany the first form of any work. For, whatever the author may say, several to whom the truth (of my just resentment) is not unknown, could not see these impertinences without making some judgment to my disadvantage. Wishing to prevent which, it has seemed to me necessary to delay no longer in bringing to light, not an imperfect, newly scribbled document, but one which is entirely completed, and which I have kept for a long time fully ready for publication.

But, my Lord, as it were, the things which are by nature unusual, need to find support in an authority which is not ordinary. This book, being of this nature (with regard to its invention), could not see day more happily than under the protection of a Lord whose virtues are esteemed and admired by all.

That is why I am resolved, in giving it to the eyes and judgment of all, to provide for it powerful protection, by the offer which I make to your Excellency. Assured, by the perfection with which your Excellency has acquitted himself, that the affection which you have shown for this subject, could not but be favourable to an ambition which has taken as its object the service of the public, and which I

❖ LE MARQVIS DE BUCKINGHAM

Cest pourquoy ie me suis resolu le donnant aux yeux & iugement de tous, de le pouruoir d'une puissante protection, par l'offre que i'en fais a vostre Grandeur, assuré que l'affection quelle a tesmoigné auoir a son subiect par la perfection quelle sen est a quise, ne la pourroit rendre que fauourable a vne ambition qui a pris pour obiect l'vtilité d'un public & laquelle ie desire passionnement (Monseignevr) *estre suiuie d'une occasion ou mon affection & ma vie se portent ensemble pour marque que ie m'estime né pour mourir.*

De Vostre Grandeur
 Le tres humble & tres obeissant seruiteur,
         F. De Lauze.

TO MY LORD BUCKINGHAM

passionately desire, my Lord, shall be followed by an opportunity where my affection and my life unite to testify that which I consider myself born to die for.

      Your Lordship's
          Very humble and very obedient servant,
                            F. DE LAUZE.

A LVYMESME

LA *cour se va mouuent aux regles de ta danse,*
 L'Amour du hault des Cieux t'es leue des autelz,
 Et Venus animee, au son de ta cadence,
 Te prepare vn palais au rang des immortelz.

I. F.

TO HIMSELF

T HE Court moves to the rules of thy dance,
   Love from high heavens raises altars to thee,
   And Venus enlivened by the sound of thy cadence,
   Prepares for thee a Palace in the ranks of the Immortals.

I. F.

ADUERTISSEMENT

LECTEVR, *encore que ie croye ce que les doctes m'ont apris,* que tout bien est communicable, & *que l'experience face voir que l'on a de tout temps hay la memoire de ceux qui ont emporté les aduantages qu'ils auoient eu du Ciel dans leur tombeau, si est-ce que ce mien trauail, (dont ie recognois le suiect meriter vne meilleure plume que la mienne) n'eust de ma vie sorty des tenebres où ie l'auois confiné, si le trait d'vne ame trop ambitieuse forçant mon silence, ne m'eust obligé de faire iour aux imperfections de mon esprit & de mon stile, pour rappeller ma reputation que mes amis trouuoient, engagee dans vne iniure insuportable.*

Sçache donc qu'il y a trois ans que fraischement arriué en Angleterre ie communiquay au sieur Montagut le dessain que i'auois de faire quelque chose sur la danse, & luy laissant vne coppie de ce que i'en auois desia trassé, le priay de la considerer & me conseiller en amy s'il seroit à propos que ie passasse outre: Il ne l'eut pas si tost veuë que loüant infiniment ma premiere resolution il me tentoit par mille flateuses paroles a la poursuitte de cest œuure, dont il protestoit souhaitter l'accomplissement auec impatience, & qui seroit indubitablement (disoit-il) bien veu de tout le monde, me faisant deslors sentir que ses persuasions ne tendoient qu'à son aduantage, & que sa vanite se promettoit cela de ma franchise que ie luy cederois aisement tout l'honneur qui se pourroit tirer de mes peines.

Quelques mois apres luy disant que i'y auois mis la

NOTICE

R EADER,
Although I believe what the learned taught me, that "all good can be communicated", and that experience shows that one has at all times hated the memory of those who have taken with them, to their graves, the advantages which they had had from Heaven. The fact is, however, that this, my work, of which I recognise the subject deserves a better pen than mine, would never have emerged, during my lifetime, from the darkness where I had confined it, if the trick of a too ambitious soul had not forced my silence, had not obliged me to bring to light the imperfections of my intelligence and my style, in order to save my reputation, which my friends found involved in an insufferable insult.

Know then that three years ago, having newly arrived in England, I communicated to Mr. Montague that I intended to execute something on the dance, and, leaving him a copy of what I had already written, I begged him to consider it, and to advise me, as a friend, if I should proceed. He had barely seen it than, praising my former resolution exceedingly, he tempted me by a thousand flattering words to pursue this work, of which he professed to desire the completion with impatience, and which, he said, would undoubtedly be well received by everyone, making me feel from then on that his persuasions only tended to his own advantage. Furthermore, that his vanity hoped that, by my frankness, I would readily yield to him all the credit which I could obtain from my work.

Telling him, some months later, that I had finished the last corrections, and even letting him see a discourse which

ADUERTISSEMENT

derniere main, & mesme luy faisant voir vn discours que i'y auois adiousté en faueur de mon subiect, il n'oublia pas vn de ses artifices pour tirer de moy & faire imprimer en son nom ce que je n'auois pas assez d'asseurance de donner au public; Mais ses prieres, ses promesses & toutes ses importunitez demeurans nulles, il recherca d'autres moyens que ie tais, & desquels ceux qui les sçauent ne peuuent parler qu'à sa confusion. En fin la longueur du temps non plus que la raison n'ayant peu matter ceste ambition qu'il auoit de triompher du merite d'vn autre, il fist dernierement transcrire sans aucune alteration, la coppie qu'il tenoit de moy & la feit grossir d'vn certain discours qu'il intitule Loüange de la Danse, *& dont l'Autheur a vne entiere obligation à Agrippa en ses Paradoxes de l'incertitude & abus des Sciences.*

En cest aueuglement il a presenté comme sienne ceste rare piece de rapport, à Monseigneur le Marquis de Buckingham, donnant par là subject à toute la Cour, (qui cognoist la fourbe) de s'entretenir pour vn temps sur ceste gentille inuention de gloire, & à moy qui suis interessé de te marquer icy en suitte des ressentimens que ie doibs à ceste iniure, la honte que merite celuy à qui il a fié son affaire: Car i'aduoüe franchement qu'il a trop de suffisance en sa profession, & n'ay pas son esprit en si mauuaise estime pour m'imaginer qu'il se soit peu luy mesme embarasser dans de si lourdes impertinences, que celles qui se voyent en la confrontation de son liure & du mien, & desquelles son second ne se sçauroit excuser, qui me pardonnera si ie dis, qu'il a esté en cela peu fidelle ou peu iudicieux.

Car de s'obliger de traicter de la Methode pour les Dames, & n'en rien dire du tout: Promettre d'enseigner en son lieu deux ou trois sortes de reuerences, &

NOTICE

I had added in favour of my subject, he did not omit a single manœuvre to extract from me, and to have printed in his own name, that which I had not had sufficient assurance to give to the public. But his prayers, his promises, and all his importunities being of no avail, he sought other means, which I will pass over, and which those who know of them can only speak of to his confusion. Finally, when neither the passage of time nor reason having been able to abate this ambition of his, whereby he desired to triumph through the merits of another, he had transcribed recently, without any alteration, the copy which he had had from me. This he augmented by a certain discourse, which he called "In Praise of the Dance", of which the author is entirely indebted to Agrippa in his Paradoxes of uncertainty and abuse of the Sciences.

In this blindness, he has presented, as his own, this singular patch-work to my Lord, the Marquess of Buckingham, thus giving to the whole Court (who knew of the deception) occasion to entertain themselves for a time by this nice device for fame. As for me, who am interested to show you, in consequence of the resentment that I owe to this injury, the shame deserved by him to whom one has entrusted his affairs. Because I admit frankly that he has too much ability in his profession, and I do not hold his intelligence in such low esteem as to imagine that he will not be somewhat embarrassed by such great impertinences such as those which are seen when his and my book are compared, the which cannot be excused by his second, and who will pardon me if I say that, in this, he has been scarcely accurate or judicious.

For to be obliged to treat on the Method for Ladies, and not to mention it at all; to promise to teach in their place two or three sorts of curtsies, and of this no word; to mention only the first three *Bransles* very lightly, and to refer to a fuller discourse which he has made on the others, with an

ADUERTISSEMENT

de cela nulles nouuelles, ne parler que des trois premiers bransles fort legerement & renuoyer à vn discours plus ample qui s'en fait auec les autres, à vne inuisible Methode pour les Dames: donner en fin à vne piece imparfaicte, le tiltre de ce qu'il faut obseruer à la Danse pour en acquerir la perfection, sans les autres absurditez que pour n'estre ennuyeux ie laisse à remarquer à ceux qui en voudront prendre la peine, sont des apparences visibles que le Sieur Montagut a esté mal seruy pour son argent, lequel ne deuoit iamais pour son honneur auoir tant de creance à ce qui sortoit des mains de ce Copiste, que d'en mespriser la veuë, pour en effacer au moins ce qui pourroit asseurer le soubçon qu'il sçauoit bien deuoir naistre de ceste sienne charité enuers moy: Mais son genie luy en a joüé d'vne ce coup là, permettant à sa vanité de trahir son iugement.

NOTICE

invisible Method for Ladies; to give, in fact, an imperfect work the title of "What must be observed in the Dance to acquire Perfection", without the other absurdities which, in order not to be tedious, I will leave to others to remark on who like to take the trouble, that these are obvious signs that Mr. Montague has been badly served for his money. He ought never, for his honour, to have given so much credence to that which left the hands of the copyist as to despise looking it over, in order to efface at least that which would have allayed the suspicions which he knew well must arise from this, his charity, towards me. But his genius played him a bad turn there, permitting his vanity to betray his judgment.

PREFACE

────◆◆◆◆◆◆────

Ie m'amusois vn iour à considerer d'où procedoit le malheur de plusieurs qui escriuent, que ceux en faueur de qui ils ont employé vne bonne partie de leur vie, ne payent ordinairement tant de sueurs & de veilles que de mocquerie & d'ingratitude, & apres auoir pezé les raisons que ie croyois la cause de ceste iniurieuse mescognoissance; ie n'en trouuay point de plus forte que ceste naturelle dispatie qui a de tout téps tyrannisé les humeurs des hommes, & qui a donné credit à ce vieil dire, autant d'aduis que de testes. *On me dira qu'il n'apartient pas à tout le monde de faire des liures, qu'il ne faut pas mettre au iour ses fantasies mal à propos, & qu'auant que les coucher à la presse il les faut esprouuer, & sans effronterie sonder si on aura autant d'asseurance que le papier: en fin que ceux qui postposent toute autre consideration à celle de se faire cognoistre ce n'est pas merueilles s'ils sont cogneus à leur desaduantage, & si la bonne opinion qu'on auoit de leur esprit s'est alterée quand on l'a veu marqué d'ancre.*

Ie ne mets point toutes ces choses en debat elles sont sans replique, & ne suis pas de ceux qui sacrifieroient à l'impertinence, mais de n'espargner pas mesmes tant de braues gens qui ont si long temps & si heureusement conuerse sur ceste montaigne tant renommée du Dieu des sciences, & qui ont si dignement traité ce qu'ils ont entrepris, que me peut-on respondre, sinon que comme chasque chose tend à son centre, de mesme nostre inclination par le mal-heur auquel nous engagea la desobeissance premiere se porte naturellement au mal,

PREFACE

I WAS amusing myself one day by considering whence proceeded the misfortune of some who write, that those in favour of whom they have employed a great part of their life only reward so much toil and vigil by mockery and ingratitude. Thus having dwelt upon the reasons which I believed to be the cause of this wrongful ingratitude, I found nothing so strong as the natural aversion which has at all times tyrannised the tempers of men, and which has given credit to the old saying, "As many opinions as heads". It will be said that it is not fitting for everyone to write books. That people should not bring to light their fancies unseasonably, and that before setting them in the press, these should be proved and, without impudence, examined thoroughly, so that they shall have as much confidence as the paper aspires to. Those, therefore, who put aside all other consideration to that of becoming known, it is scarcely remarkable if they are discovered to their disadvantage, and the good opinion that one had had of their wit is altered when one has seen it appear in print.

I do not put all these things to debate; they are unanswerable. Also I am not among those who sacrifice to impertinence. But I do not spare likewise many worthy people who have conversed so long and happily upon this mountain, so greatly renowned of the God of the Sciences, and who have so justly discoursed upon that which they have undertaken. What can they answer me? Except that as each thing tends towards its centre, so likewise, through the misfortune by which we invite the first disobedience, our inclination is disposed naturally to evil, as to its most

PREFACE

comme à son obiect plus souhaitable, où elle se lie si estroitement que nous ne l'en pouuons separer que par violence, ie veux dire par vne soigneuse estude de la vertu qui pressupose tousiours du contraste.

Mais d'autant que la deprauation de nostre nature nous fait trouuer ce combat trop penible, il est extraordinaire de voir quelqu'vn qui ne se laisse emporter à l'influence de son astre, ce que n'ignorant pas, ce seroit perdre la cognoissance de moy mesme, de m'imaginer pouuoir estre plus heureux qu'vne infinité de beaux esprits, qui ont esté mis au monde pour y estre admirez de mes semblables, & qui pourtant ne se sont peu affranchir de l'agitation de tant de vents contraires.

Ie sçay donc bien que ceste mienne entreprise donnera pour vn temps de l'entretien aux partisans d'Aristarque, & ne suis pas en doubte qu'elle n'apporte quand & soy de l'estonnement à tout ceux qui me cognoissent, quand ils verront vn effect bien different de celuy qu'ils deuroient attendre de ma nourriture & du premier train de ma vie, mais ceux la cognoistront par le peu de crainte que ie tesmoigne auoir de la caiolerie, que i'ay preferé au mespris & à la mesdisance de quelques vns, l'enuie de proffiter à tous, & ie supplie les autres de considerer, que ce n'est pas vn vice de nous seruir d'vn honneste aduantage lors que la fortune ou l'infortune nous y oblige.

Il est vray, ce n'est pas mon mestier que la danse, ny certes ma resolution de mourir en l'exerçant, mais en vn temps & en vn pays où ie me trouue engagé de mettre en pratique ce que pousse de mon inclination i'auois autre fois appris pour mon contentement particulier, & par maniere d'exercice, c'est ma gloire de m'en pouuoir aquitter sciemment, & contenter ensemble ceux qui m'imitent, & cest essay me seruira de

PREFACE

desirable object, where it is so firmly bound that we cannot disentangle ourselves from it, except with a struggle. I mean to say, through a careful study of the faculty which always presupposes a contrast.

But forasmuch as the depravity of our natures makes us find this struggle too hard, it is uncommon to see someone who does not let himself be swayed by the influence of his planet. Not to be aware of which would be to lose the understanding of myself, to imagine myself able to be more fortunate than an infinity of wits who have been put into the world in order to be admired by my fellow-men, and who, for all that, have scarcely become free from the agitation of so many adverse opinions.

I know full well that this, mine enterprise, will, for a time, give some discourse to the partisans of Aristarchus. And I am in no doubt that it will astonish all those who know me, when they see a result very different from that which they would have expected from my livelihood and from my early way of life. But they will know me by the little regard that I have for flattery, as I have preferred to bear the contempt and slanders of some in the desire to benefit all. I entreat others to consider that it is not a vice to avail ourselves of an honest advantage, when fortune, or ill-fate, obliges us.

It is true that the dance is not my only calling, nor certainly is it my resolution to die in exercising it. But at a time and in a country where I find myself compelled to put into practice that which springs from my inclination, and which I had previously learnt for my particular amusement and as a manner of exercising, it is my boast to be able to acquit myself in it knowingly, and at the same time to satisfy those who follow me. This essay will serve to vouch for me that vanity never gives me these words, because whosoever attempts the practice of what follows will realise its necessity, for he will only meet with actions in

PREFACE

garand que la vanité ne me donne point ces paroles, car quiconque entrera en quelque experience de son vtilité, il n'y rencontrera que des actions, ou la bien seance se remarquera tousiours, comme en son element plus necessaire.

Que si quelque esprit de contradiction, (comme il est presque impossible autrement pour les raisons que i'ay dictes) se iette icy à la trauerse, & blasonne ce que i'escris, ie me console en ce qu'il ne le peut faire qu'au desaduantage des plus renommez de la profession, qui pratiquent ceste Methode, & ausquels ie fais vn sacrifice volontaire de ma peine & du desir extreme que i'ay, que la danse possedant l'honneur qu'elle merite, fut autant estimée comme elle est estimable: Ce qui semble ne pouuoir iamais estre qu'au prealable on ne l'aye tirée de dessous les pieds de l'ignorance, qui la gehenne & la contrainct à des postures indignes d'estre veuës, bien moins d'estre imitées.

C'est pourquoy si i'estois creu, on obserueroit desormais ceste regle, que nul ne pourroit auoir liberté de monstrer soit en public ou en particulier sans le certificat de quelques vns qui seroient choisis à cest effect, deuant lesquels il seroit obligé de rendre des preuues de la iustesse de ses actions, ensemble de sa suffisance, ou si incapable renuoyé a l'escole, procedure qui donneroit sans doubte vne loüable enuie à plusieurs d'employer heureusement leur temps, & à d'autres de corriger les deffauts où leur aueuglement (causé de trop de licence) les a entretenus iusques icy. Voila franchement mon opinion, laquelle si elle n'est pas suiuie, il ne s'ensuit pas qu'elle ne le deust estre, bien asseuré qu'on ne me peut accuser en cela que de trop d'affection, qui sera peut-estre vn iour secondée de quelque autre moins malheureuse & plus authorisee.

C'est à vous Messieurs qui y auez de l'interest, de

PREFACE

which good behaviour will always be noticeable as the most necessary element.

If some contradictory opinion throws itself against it (which, for the reasons I have said, is nearly impossible to avoid) and criticises that which I write, I console myself in that this will only be done to the disadvantage of the more renowned of the profession who practise this Method. To them I make a voluntary sacrifice of my labour, from the great desire that I have that the dance shall possess the honour that it merits, to be as much esteemed as it is estimable. This it seems could never be, if as a preliminary one did not extricate it from under the feet of ignorance, which impedes and constrains it in postures unworthy to be seen, much less to be imitated.

For this reason, if I were believed, one should observe hereafter this rule: that none should have the liberty of teaching, whether in public or in private, without a certificate from people who would be chosen for this purpose, before whom it would be obligatory to render some proof of the justness of their actions, together with their capability. Or, if incapable, that they be sent back to school. Procedure which would give, without doubt, a laudable desire to many to employ their time well, and to others to correct the faults where their blindness (caused by too much liberty) has taken them up to now. That is frankly my opinion, which, if it is not followed, does not signify that it ought not to be, being well assured myself that no one can accuse me of too much affectation in this, which perhaps will one day be supported by some other less unfortunate and of more authority.

It is for you, gentlemen, who have an interest in it, to give henceforth a better warrant for the continuance of your reputation than the tacit consent which it seems you give to the abuses (by your sufferance), thus bearing it to the same tomb where the negligence of our predecessors

PREFACE

donner desormais vn meilleur ordre à la duree de vostre reputation que le tacite consentement, qu'il semble que vous donnez aux abus (par vostre souffrance) va portant dans le mesme tombeau ou la negligence de nos deuanciers a mis l'origine des Danses, dont la recherche seroit inutile: car nostre malheur est tel que nous n'en auons quasi rien de certain. Ce que i'en ay peu apprendre se voit chez Scaliger, *qui asseure y auoir autre fois eu quatre sortes de Danses, vne fort graue appellée* Emelie, *vne gaye dicte* Cordax, *vne autre qui mesloit à la gayeté quelque graue contenance & se nommoit* Siccenix, *la derniere s'appelloit* Perrichie *ou danse armee ainsi dicte d'vn certain* Pirrhus *qui en fut l'inuenteur, & ces danses ont depuis esté comparees aux modernes par* Arena Prouençal, *sçauoir l'*Emelie, *aux Pauanes & Bassedãses tãt reguliere qu'irreguliere, le* Cordax, *aux Gaillardes, Tordions & Voltes, le* Siccenix *aux Bransles, la* Perrichie *aux Bouffons & Matassins, & c'est ceste cy que les Saliens instituez par* Numa *dansoient au nombre de douze aux festes Sacrees de Bellonne.*

Il faut au surplus remarquer que de tout temps en chasque contree ou Prouince on a eu vne danse affectee, comme les Anglois les mesures & contredanses, les Escossois les Bransles d'Escosse, les Alemans l'Alemande, les Normans les Bransles de village, les Bretons le Triory ou Passepied, les Bransles de Poitou viennent des Poiteuins, & la Volte de Prouence, des Italiens la Gaillarde ou Romanesque, des Espagnols la Sarabande & Pauane, des Mores les Morisques, à Paris & plusieurs autres lieux de la France, nous auons la diuersité des Bransles & Courantes tant à figures que simples auec partie des susdites danses. Quant aux Canaries elles y sont aussi fort en vsage,

PREFACE

laid the origin of the dance, whereof research would be useless. For our ill luck is such that we have in this almost nothing certain. That whereof I have learnt a little can be seen in *Scaliger*, who affirms having had in earlier times four kinds of dances. A grave kind called *Emelie*; a gay, said to be *Cordax*; another which mixed with the gay some grave contents, and was named *Siccenix*. The last was called *Perrochie*, or the armed dance, thus named after a certain Pirrhus, who was its inventor. These dances have since been compared with the modern ones by Arena, a Provençal. That is to say, the *Emelie* to the *Pavanes*, and *Bassedanses*, as well the "regular" as the "irregular". The *Cordax* to the *Gaillardes*, *Tordions*, and *Voltes*. The *Siccenix* to the *Bransles*, the *Perrichis* to the *Bouffons* and *Matassins*. And it is this one which the Salii, instituted by Numa, danced to the number of twelve at the feasts sacred to Bellona.

One must remark, furthermore, that at all times and in each district, or Province, one has had a given dance, such as the English have measures and *contredances*. The Scottish have the *Scotch Brawl*, the Germans the *Almain*, the Normans the *Bransles-de-villages*, the Bretons the *Triory*, or *Passepied*. The *Bransles de Poitou* come from the Poitevins, and the *Volta* from Provence. From the Italians come the *Gaillarde*, or *Romanesque*. From the Spaniards the *Sarabande* and *Pavane*. From the Moors the *Morisco*. From Paris, and some other places in France, we have a diversity of the *Bransles* and *Courantes*, both figured and simple, with parts of the above-named dances. As for the *Canaries*, they are also greatly in use, but their origin is uncertain. Some say that in the isles of this name this dance is common, but I prefer the following opinion; that such as many of our airs of the *Courante* have been taken from some *Balets*, the *Canaries* came also from a *Balet* where the dancers represented the Kings and Queens of Mauritania, disguised as savages and covered with feathers of divers colours. If any-

PREFACE

mais leur origine est incertaine, les vns disent qu'aux Isles de ce nom là ceste danse est ordinaire, mais i'ayme mieux ceste opinion, que comme plusieurs de nos airs de Courante ont esté tirez de quelques Balets, les Canaries viennent aussi d'vn Balet où les Danseurs representoient les Roys & Reynes de Mauritanie desguisez en Sauuages couuerts de plumages de diuerses couleurs. Si quelqu'vn en desire sçauoir dauantage Arbeau m'a promis de se seruir de son Orchesographie pour me soulager de ceste peine là les curieux trouueront quelque chose digne de leur enuie où ie les lairay aller pour venir où mon dessein m'appelle.

PREFACE

one wishes to know more of this, Arbeau has promised me to make use of his *Orchésographie* in order to relieve me of this work. There the curious will find something worthy of their interest, whither I will let them resort in order to proceed where my purpose summons me.

APOLOGIE DE LA DANSE

I'AY *balancé long-temps si ie lairrois eschapper de mes mains ce traicté, pour l'incertitude de la reüssie de ma peine, attendu la qualité du sujet dont ie parle, & la diuersité de tant d'esprits qui choquent ordinairement ce qui n'est pas de leur humeur, dont les vns croyront (peut-estre) que ie veux authoriser vn Paradoxe, les autres que i'entreprends d'adiouster des appas & des attraicts au vice, parmy des ames qui y ont desia assez d'inclination naturelle, qu'vne longue habitude leur a fortifiée, & que les occasions ordinaires & les mauuais exemples resueilleroient si elle estoit endormie.*

Mais les premiers seront aisement satisfaits s'ils se donnent la patience de voir surquoy ie me fonde, & pour ne les enuyer, ie ne les entretiendray point des fables de la Poësie, ie n'appelleray point à tesmoin vn Arion *qui au son de sa voix & de la lire fist iadis danser ce Dauphin qui le deliura du naufrage, ny cest* Orphée *qui trouuoir en toutes choses vne si grande disposition à la danse, que les inanimées mesmes se ioignoyent au bal, animées des charmes de sa lire: & ne tireray point ma consequence de l'ordre qu'on donne à la nature de ceste admirable proportiõ des causes, ny de ceste* Symmetrie, *par laquelle les Cieux, les Elemens, & tant de choses de soy contraires & disioinctes, sont par vn accord discordant, & cadence miraculeuse vnies & conseruées en cest assemblage & continuité de l'Vniuers, auquel les Stoiciens (rauis de tant de merueilles) ont donné vn corps & vne ame, l'estimant estre vn animal de nature immortelle ie*

AN APOLOGY FOR THE DANCE

I HAVE hesitated a long while whether I should let this treatise escape from my hands, for the uncertainty of the success of my labour, seeing the nature of the subject of which I speak, and the diversity of so many opinions, which are shocked ordinarily by that which is not to their liking. Some, perhaps, will believe that I wish to authorise a Paradox and others that I undertake to add to the allurements and attractions of vice among those persons who already have enough natural inclination. Long habit having so strengthened this in them that customary opportunities and evil precedent would awaken it in them if it were dormant.

But the first will be easily satisfied if they have the patience to see that whereon I base my views. In order not to weary them, I will not hold forth on the fables of Poetry. I shall not call to witness one Arion, who, to the sound of his voice and his lyre, in old times made that Dolphin dance who delivered him from the shipwreck. Neither do I forget Orpheus, who found in all things so great a disposition to dance that even inanimate objects joined in the dance, animated by the charms of his lyre. I will not draw my conclusions about the pattern which one usually attributes to Nature on this admirable proportion of the Causes. Nor by that Symmetry by which the Skies, the Elements and many things, of themselves contrary and disunited, are by a discordant agreement miraculously harmonised, united, and conserved in this union and continuity of the Universe. The Stoics, enchanted by so many marvels, have given it a body and a soul, estimating it to be an animal of immortal nature. I will leave this matter for the study of some Poet,

❖ APOLOGIE *de la* DANSE

lairray ceste matiere pour l'exercice de quelque Poëte, & les prieray de considerer auec moy, que les plus remarquables personnages de toute l'antiquité, ie dis & sacrez & profanes, ont honoré la danse, & de voix & de pratique. Ceux là me fourniroyent vne multitude d'exemples, si la reuerence que ie porte au liure de Dieu, me permettoit le meslange des choses sainctes à celles qui ne le sont pas, joint aussi que ie m'engagerois d'expliquer le sens des Escritures, pour faire voir le suject qui obligeoit tant de sainctes ames à la danse, ce qui contrarie à la briefueté que ie me suis proposée, vn autre dira à ma capacité, ie l'aduouë: Mais si est-ce qu'il n'y a rien de plus palpable que les plus authorisez parmy le peuple de Dieu (poussez d'vne saincte allegresse) ont dansé, & que depuis en la primitiue Eglise, la coustume longtemps continuée a esté, qu'on obseruoit des cadences & des pas mesurez au son de certains motetz qu'on y chantoit. Que si on me dit la dessus que la difference du danser de ces anciennes Eglises, à celuy de nos bals & de nos assemblées (qu'on feint autante de tendez-vous en faueur de l'entretien du vice,) aneantit l'authorité que ie recherche en vne coustume dans le retranchement de laquelle se voit enseuelie toute la consequence que i'en pourrois tirer, si ne me peut on nier toutes fois que ces vieilles façons de faire & la souffrance de nos anciés Orthodoxes n'authorisent assez que la danse en soy ne peut estre blasmable, & c'est ce que ie demande.

 Qu'ils viennent donc auec moy chez les Profanes, & ie leur fairay cognoistre qu'vn Socrates (à qui ce fameux oracle d'Apollon donna la qualité de tressage) a prit à danser d'Aspasia, & que son disciple le diuin Platon conseille de ne pas employer moins de temps, & de solicitude aux exercices du corps qu'à ceux de l'ame: il ne veut pas qu'on les esleue l'vn sans l'autre:

and pray others to consider, with me, that the most remarkable personages of all antiquity, I mean both sacred and profane, have honoured the dance by both voice and practice. These would furnish me with a multitude of examples, if the reverence that I have for the Book of God permitted me to mix things Holy with those which are not. Added to that, in order to make the subject understood, I would take upon myself to explain the sense of the Scriptures which obliged so many Saintly people to dance. That which is contrary to the brevity which I intend, another could say to the limit of my capacity, I own. But is it not true that there is nothing more palpable than that the most authorised amongst the people of God, forced by Holy joy, have danced, since the custom continued for a long time in the early Church, whereby they observed certain cadences and measured steps to the sound of certain motets that were sung there. If they tell me, thereupon, that the difference between the dance of these ancient Churches and that of our balls and assemblies, which they make believe will lead you in favour of entertaining vice, annihilates the authority which I seek for in a custom, in the suppression of which is seen buried all the consequence I am able to infer, nevertheless they are unable to gainsay me that these old ceremonies, also the sufferance of our ancient orthodoxies, only warrants sufficient proof that the dance itself cannot be blameworthy, and it is this that I ask.

Let them come then with me to the Profane Ones, and I will make known to them that one, Socrates (to whom the famous oracle of Apollo gave the quality of great wisdom), took Aspasia to dance. Also that his disciple, the divine Plato, counselled that no less time and solicitude be employed in the exercise of the body than in that of the mind. He did not wish that one should exalt the one without the other, but that they should be conducted equally, like a pair of Horses harnessed to the same carriage-pole. Among

mais qu'on les conduise esgallement comme vne couple de Cheuaux attelez à mesme timon, & entre les diuertissemens qu'il a donnez à l'ame, tant s'en faut qu'il aye oublié la danse, qu'il ordonne mesmes aux vieillards d'y assister, non pour imiter la ieunesse: mais pour se resiouyr en autruy & rappeller à leur souuenance la grace & ferueur de leur aage verdissant, C'est merueille combien il est soigneux en ses loix de leurs courses, ieux & danses, desquelles il dit que l'ancienneté a donné la conduicte & patronnage aux Dieux mesmes, bien contraire en cela, à la pluspart de nos Pedans, lesquels (comme s'ils auoyent conspiré contre la gentillesse du corps) souffrent seulement à leurs Escoliers certains exercices qui ne les peuuent entretenir que dans l'ineptie, presque inseparable de ceux qui suyuent le train de leur institution, & leur deffendent la pratique d'autres qui les façonneroyent & les rendroit dignes d'vne ciuile conuersation, de laquelle vne si impertinente police les bannit ou les y fait receuoir comme des buses pour seruir de suject à la raillerie: Mais on a beau dire, ces Messieurs n'altereront pas pour cela la nature de leurs Colleges, & ne souscriront iamais que la science de l'antregent soit necessaire à la ieunesse, on ne leur ostera point cest erreur, que les exercices qui seruent le plus à ceste sçience ne soient autant d'allechemens à la desbauche, leur ignorance est en cela fatalement affectee; Or d'autant qu'il n'y à rien à gaigner auec des gens, qui ne se peuuent separer de la passion mauuaise conseillere en toutes choses, & d'ailleurs que ie ne voudrois pas m'esloigner de mon subiect par vne disgretion trop estenduë, retournant à ceux à qui ie parlois premierement ie les prieray de me suiure, pour leur faire voir que ie puis adiouster à l'authorité de Socrates & de Platon celle de plusieurs claires lumieres de l'anti-

the diversions which he has given for the people, so far from having forgotten the dance, he enjoined the old to assist, not in order to imitate the young, but in order to rejoice in others and to recall to their remembrance the grace and fervour of their green years. It is a wonder how mindful he is in his rules for their races, games, and dances, of which he said that Antiquity had given the conduct and patronage even to the Gods. Quite contrary to the greater part of our Pedants, who (as if they had conspired against the elegance of the body) only suffer their Scholars to do certain exercises which can only preserve in them that ineptitude which is almost inseparable in those who follow the way of their school, and which forbids them to practise other methods which would fashion them, and render them worthy of a civil conversation, from which such impertinent conduct banishes them, or at least makes them accepted as butts to serve as a subject for mockery. But in spite of what is said, these Gentlemen will not alter the nature of their Colleges for all that, and will never admit that the science of Civility should be necessary to youth; for one will never remove this error from their thinking, that the exercises which render the most service to this science will not be so many enticements to debauchery. Their ignorance in this is fatally affected. Now, seeing that there is nothing to be gained from these people, who are unable to separate themselves from passion, which is a bad counsellor in all things, I do not, moreover, wish to depart from my subject by a too extensive digression. So, in returning to those to whom I will speak firstly, I pray them to follow me, in order to make them see that I can add to the authority of Socrates and Plato that of many shining lights of pagan antiquity. Homer will tell them, in my favour, that assemblies and feasts cannot be enlivened except by the dance. I will show them in Plutarch that one, Damonides, has put it among the ranks of the more commendable things, and that Epamin-

APOLOGIE *de la* DANSE

quité payenne. Homere leur dira en ma faueur que les assemblées & les festins font vn corps qui ne peut estre animé que de la danse. Ie leur monstreray dans Plutarque qu'vn Damonidas l'a mise au rang des choses plus recommãdables, & qu'Epaminondas s'en seruoit industrieusement au choc d'vne bataille, & s'y exerçoit encores parmy les dames de sa cité, n'estimant pas que ce fut chose qui derogeast à l'honneur de ses victoires ny à la reformation de sa vie. Ils verront en Xenophon qu'on honnora de dãses & mascarades l'arriuee des Capitaines de Cyrus: & en Macrobe que les enfans des Senateurs de Rome au sortir des escoles aloient apprendre à danser.

Ie ioindrois à ceux cy vne infinité d'autres & aux anciens les modernes, si ceux qui ne se lairront pas dessiller les yeux à la veuë de ces soleils ne deuoient par consequant mespriser toute autre lumiere. Qu'vn plus opiniastre que moy s'essaye de les persuader, ie ne perdray pas ainsi & mon temps & ma peine, ny ne m'amuseray encores à redire ce qu'Atheneus, Celius, Scaliger, Lucian, Iulius Polux, & tant d'autres ont assez amplement escript, qui tous demeurent d'accord que la danse outre qu'elle est grandement necessaire à la conseruation de la santé; n'est pas moins agreable aux vieux, que conuenable aux ieunes, & bien seante à quiconque se voudra tenir au dedans de la modestie. C'est vne eloquence muete que Roscius fit iadis aduouer bien plus forte & plus persuasiue que celle de Ciceron, à qui le despit d'auoir esté condamné par les arbitres augmenta de beaucoup la douleur que luy causoient les vlceres de les iambes.

Voila la satisfaction où ie me suis insensiblement engagé pour le contentement de ceux que ie disois au commencement de ce discours me vouloir peut-estre soubçonner de quelque extrauagance qui cederont

An APOLOGY for the DANCE

ondas himself used it skilfully in the shock of battle, and exercised it also among the ladies of the city, not considering that this was a thing which was derogatory to the honour of his victories, neither to the reformation of his life. They will see in Xenophon that they honoured the arrival of the Captains of Cyrus with dances and masquerades, and in Macrobe that the children of the Senators of Rome, on leaving school, went to learn to dance.

I could add to these an infinity of others, both ancient and modern, therefore those who do not let their eyes be opened to the sight of these suns, ought not, in consequence, to despise all other light. Let one more stubborn than I try to persuade them, so that I shall not thereby be deprived either of my time or my labour, neither amuse myself furthermore in retelling that which *Atheneus, Celius, Scaliger, Lucian, Julius Polux*, and many others have amply enough written. All were of one accord that the dance, besides being greatly necessary for the preservation of health, is not less agreeable to the old than suitable to the young, and is becoming to whomsoever wishes to maintain modesty therein. As Roscius has admitted of old, it is a mute eloquence, even stronger and more persuasive than that of *Cicero*, to whom the vexation of having been condemned by the judges augmented greatly the pain caused him by ulcers of the legs.

Behold the satisfaction whereby I am insensibly engaged for the pleasure of those who, as I said at the beginning of this discourse, were willing perhaps to suspect me of some extravagance, but who, doubtless, will give way to the force of reason, authority, and experience.

As for the others of whom I spoke thereafter, I protest that their considerations (although even more unfavourable) are too slight to deprive me of the desire to acquit myself of that which I believe I owe to the good of the well-

sans doubte à la force de la raison, de l'authorité & de l'experience.

Pour les autres dont ie parlois en suitte, ie proteste que leurs considerations, (quoy que plus des aduantageuses) sont trop legeres pour me faire perdre l'enuie de m'aquiter de ce que ie pense deuoir au bien d'vne noblesse bien née, qui sçait comme moy qu'on ne manque point de rencontrer des esprits qui choisiront plustost l'escart de quelques sinistres opinions, que le grand chemin d'vne verité toute battuë? Ie sçay bien qu'ils se mocqueront des authoritez dont ie m'appuie, mais ie sçay bien aussi que ce sera le renuier par dessus Epimenides qui dressa des autels à l'impudense, quoy qu'ils dient, ils ne m'empecheront point de suiure mon dessein, & me soucie fort peu d'estre en butte de leur medisance.

Ie n'entre pas aussi en debat auec certains personnages mal taillez & difformes qui ne peuuent cacher les deffauts qu'ils ont de la nature qu'en la ruine de la bien seance, non plus qu'auec ceux qui comme des Timons se sont retirez de la societé des hommes, pour viure gras & ingrats, & donner la chasse aux Chimeres: l'enuie pousse ceux-là au mespris de la danse, pour n'auoir pas le corps disposé à receuoir les graces qui ne peuuent estre en leur perfection sans elle, & ie recuse ceux cy pource qu'ils sont obligez de controoller (au moins en apparence) ce qui contrarie à leur proffession, ioint qu'vne nouuelle façon de viure leur alterant ordinairement le ceruau & en suitte la raison, leur empesche de voir le desreglement de leurs opinions.

C'est au iugement d'arbitres non preocupez de faueur que ie m'adresse, qui aduouëront ie m'asseure que tant s'en faut que la danse aye en soy rien de blamable, qu'au contraire la bien-seance luy est vn acci-

An APOLOGY for the DANCE

born nobility, who know, as I do, that one does not fail to meet with people who would rather deviate in some sinister opinions than follow the well-beaten high road of some truth. I know well that they will mock the authorities on whom I lean, but I also know well that that would far surpass *Epimenides*, who set up altars to Impudence. Whatever they say, they will never prevent me from following my purpose, and I care very little if I become the butt of their slanders.

Neither will I enter into debate with certain badly knit and deformed persons, who could not hide the defects which they have by Nature, except by overthrowing decorum. Nor, further, with those who, like *Timons*, have withdrawn themselves from the society of men, in order to live, fat and ungrateful, and to pursue Chimeras. Envy prompts these to despise the dance, through not having a body disposed to receive the graces, and without which these graces cannot attain their full perfection. I reject these because they are obliged to censure, at least in appearance, that which is counter to their profession, which, added to a new way of living, commonly alters the brain and thereafter the reason, preventing them from seeing the distortion of their opinions.

It is to the judgment of masters who are not preoccupied with seeking favours that I address myself, who would admit, I feel assured, that the dance itself has nothing blameworthy in it. That, on the contrary, good behaviour is an inseparable element of it. Thus, though the ancients honoured it, and put it to use, having had but the shadow of the form of perfection which we possess today, it now appears that, having become more noble, it is less sought after.

Seneca said that, since Nature has given us our Being, we owe to her the study of the science of Well-Being, and I dare, without blushing, to elaborate thereupon. For the

dant inseparable. Que si les anciens l'ont honnoree & mise en vsage, n'ayant que l'ombre & la figure de la perfection que nous possedons à cest heure, qu'elle apparence qu'estant plus noble elle soit moins recherchee.

Seneque dict, que si la nature nous a donné l'estre nous sommes redeuables à l'estude de la vertu du bien estre, & i'ose sans rougir encherir là dessus que le seul exercice de la danse peut non seulement arracher les mauuaises actions qu'vne negligente nourriture auroit enracinee, mais donner encore vn maintien & vne grace que nous disons entregent, & que ie peux appeller proprement le bel estre, *chose tout à faict necessaire à quiconque veut rendre son port & son abort agreable dans le monde.*

*De façon qu'en l'ordre des choses se trouuent deux degrez (*la Philosophie & la Danse*) qui peuuent monter vn homme à sa perfection. Voici toutesfois leur difference ; c'est que le premier se peut communiquer à tous ceux qui ont de la raison sans esgard à la forme du corps, & c'est à quoy le dernier vise principalement, en fin chacun est capable de ce dont les Philosophes se ventent, & vn Canibale, mesme le plus grossier & d'esprit & de mains se peut acquerir la cognoissance de tous les arts liberaux & mecaniques, voire y peut exceller s'il y met & la peine & l'enuie, mais la danse a cela de particulier, que quiconque a le corps mal faict est incapable des graces qui l'accompagnent, il faut auoir vne matiere propre pour receuoir vne si digne forme.*

Que s'il y en a parmi ceux qui sont redeuables au ciel de ce bon heur qui se laissent porter au mespris d'vne chose qui peut empescher le mespris en bonne compagnie, ie les prie de considerer le traict d'vn de nos derniers Roys qui faisoit quelque fois admirer ses

sole exercise of the dance is able, not only to eradicate the bad actions which a negligent upbringing has ingrained, but gives also a decorum and a grace which we call Civility, and which I am able to call properly *le bel estre* (elegant presence), a thing absolutely necessary to whosoever wishes to render his deportment and his approach agreeable in society.

So that in the order of things are to be found two gradations, Philosophy and Dance, by which a man can raise himself to perfection. Yet here is their difference: that the first can be communicated to all those who have intellect, without regard to the construction of their body, which is what the last has principally in view. Finally, everyone is capable of that of which the Philosophers boast, which is that even the most primitive Cannibal can acquire, both with his mind and hands, the knowledge of all the liberal arts and mechanics, nay, even can excel therein if he gives to it both labour and zeal, but the dance has this in particular, that whomsoever has an ill-formed body is incapable of acquiring the graces which accompany it. One must have the proper material in order to receive a truly dignified bearing.

If among those who are indebted to Heaven for this good fortune there are some who allow themselves to be led to despise a thing which could turn aside the contempt of good company, I pray them to consider the description of one of our late Kings whose perfections when at a ball showed to as great an advantage over his Courtiers as he surpassed in oratory and judgment the wisest and the most eloquent of his Kingdom. He, himself, reprimanded a Gentleman (otherwise well accomplished) for not having learnt to dance, and asked of him what he *did* know how to do. "I know well, Sire," answered he, "how to give a blow of my lance in war for the service of your Majesty." "I counsel you, then," replied this good Prince, "to arm your-

APOLOGIE *de la* DANSE

perfections dans vn bal auec autant d'auantage sur ses Courtisans, comme il surpassoit en iugement & ne langue les mieux sensez & les plus eloquens de son Royaume, luy blasmant vn gentilhomme (au reste fort accompli) de n'auoir pas apris à danser, & luy demandant ce qu'il sçauoit faire, ie sçay bien, Sire, *dict-il, donner en guerre vn coup de lance pour le seruice de vostre Majesté: Ie vous conseille donc (repliqua ce braue Prince) de vous armer d'vn froc en temps de paix, comme s'il eust voulu dire que les fureurs de la guerre cessees vn Caualier ne pouuoit s'occuper à vn plus noble exercice que celuy qui luy donne vne grande entree en la cognoissance de sa Cour & de son monde.*

Mais que sert il de tant discourir en faueur d'vne chose que l'exemple des siecles passez, & les effects qu'elle produit au nostre rendent assez recommandable? pourquoy tant d'ennemis contre ce qui est si necessaire, & dequoy Messieurs nos Maistres ne me peuuent prouuer la censure dans les sainctes lettres, ouy bien dãs quelques legeres apparẽces qu'ils mettent en consideration, nous ne blasmons pas la Danse, disent-ils, pour ses pas & ses mesures, autrement la voix & la Musique courroient la mesme fortune, mais parce qu'elle oblige les Venus *à se parer plus ambitieusement, desquelles il faut fuir la hantise, d'autant que l'imagination prend feu (aussi soudain que le Naphthe) si on l'arreste tant soit peu en la contemplation d'vn obiect amoureux, qu'elle est en fin tousiours suiuie de mil mauuais desirs de vanité & de concupiscence, & ces desirs de scandales qui produisent souuent de grands malheurs.*

Ie m'estonne de ces gens qui font deux sortes de scandale (le pris & le donne,) & en condamnent l'obiect sans distinction: i'auouë que l'on doit prendre

self with a monk's robe in time of peace"; as if he wished to say that the furies of war having ceased, a gentleman could not employ himself in a more noble exercise than that which gave him an illustrious admission into the acquaintance of his Court and society.

But of what use is so much discussion in favour of a thing which the example of past centuries, and the effect which it has produced in us, renders sufficient recommendation? Why so many enemies against that which is so necessary, and of which our Masters are unable to make me establish the truth of any censure in the Scriptures, except perhaps in some slight appearances which they put for consideration? "We do not blame the Dance", say they, "for its steps and its measures, otherwise both voice and music would fare the same fortune, but because it obliges the Venuses to clothe themselves more ambitiously. One should flee from being haunted by these, for as much as the imagination takes fire, as suddenly as naphtha, if one stops even a little in the contemplation of an amorous object, and which finally is always followed by a thousand evil desires of vanity and concupiscence, and those desires for scandals, which often produce great misfortune."

I am astonished by these people, who create two kinds of scandal (that given and that taken), and who condemn a subject indiscriminately. I confess that one should beware of the one, because I do not approve that which is immodest, but who is able to prevent the other, since the Enemy of men makes use of the most innocent frankness in order to betray those susceptible to his temptations. Indeed, intention is the truest judge of our actions, if it is not impaired. Whoever would offend, he himself is the author of his offence.

But I do not wish to enter into a matter so far removed from my affairs and my purpose. I shall say, nevertheless, in passing, that those who make this a profession would

APOLOGIE *de la* DANSE

garde à l'vn, car ie n'approuue point ce qui est impudique, mais qui se peut empescher de l'autre, puis que l'ennemi des hommes se seruira des plus innocentes franchises pour trahir les ames susceptibles de ses tentations ; certes l'intention est le plus veritable iuge de nos actions, si elle n'est point alteree, peche qui voudra, il est luy mesme autheur de son offence.

Mais ie ne veux pas entrer si auant en vne matiere esloignee de mon gibier & de mon dessein, ie diray toutesfois en passant, que ceux qui en font profession employeroient plus heureusement leur plume & leur loisir à decider tant de controuerses qui tyrannisent les consciences, & dont les doutes causent vne indubitable perdition à vne infinité d'ames malheureusement forcees d'en aller demander la solution à Radamanthe, leur peine en cela seroit autant loüable, comme en ceci les iugemens biens sains la trouuent inutile.

L'authorité desquels seconde mon entreprise que ie poursuis auec d'autant plus de resolution que ie la sçay appuyee de la conformité de nos loix, & qu'elle a pour subiect vn bien tres-necessaire aux Caualiers, & aux Dames qui veulent anoblir les charmes qu'ils ont desia de la Nature, des actions & des graces qu'elle ne leur a peu donner, lesquels loüeront, ie me vante mon affection, lors que l'experience leur aura tesmoigné les effects de la methode dont ie traicte : & que ceux qui se peuuent à bon droict donner la gloire d'auoir porté la Danse parmi les choses accomplies pratiquent auiourd'huy.

Ie dis ceux : pource que ie ne puis donner ma voix à l'inconsideration de plusieurs, qui poussez de quelque affection particuliere, ou forcez, peut estre, de cest instinct qui nous faict ordinairement fauoriser vne chose plus que l'autre, & bien souuent trouuer chois

employ their pen and their leisure more happily in deciding many such controversies, which tyrannise people's consciences, doubts of which cause undoubted perdition to an infinity of people unhappily obliged to ask the solution of Rhadamanthus. Their labour in this would be the more laudable, since healthy judgments find it fruitless.

The authority which supports my enterprise, which I pursue with much more resolution since I know it to be founded in conformity with our laws, and that it has for its object a benefit very necessary for Gentlemen and for Ladies who wish to enhance the charms which they already have from Nature, by actions and graces which she has not been able to endow them with. Such will, I flatter myself, praise my inclination when experience has testified to them the effects of the method of which I treat. Also that they will be able, with good reason, to ascribe to themselves the honour of having set the Dance amidst the accomplished things which are practised today.

I say these, because I do not then give my voice to the inconsiderateness of many who, driven by some particular inclination, or forced perhaps by that instinct which we usually employ in favouring one thing more than another, and which, in a choice between two similar subjects, we very often attribute that which is advantageous to one only. Because if one recognises that many persons, whom one knows to have attained perfection in dancing well, have learnt in divers places and under different Masters, and that they themselves, by their practice and judgment, have brought to it something of their own, one will know that I have reason to say that no one person has invented all that which is accepted today as being well done. But that there are many who have more or less contributed their industry to it, and that, in consequence, it is very reasonable that even all the worthy people who honour this profession participate in this praise, if not to a like degree of honour as

en deux pareils subiects, attribuent c'est aduantage à vn seul; car si l'on iuge que tant de personnes qu'on sçait auoir attaint la perfection de bien danser, ont apris en diuers lieux & soubs differents Maistres, & qu'eux mesmes par leur exercice & iugement y ont apporté quelque chose du leur, on sçaura que i'ay raison de dire qu'vn seul n'a pas inuenté tout ce qui est auiourd'huy receu estre bien faict: mais que plusieurs, qui plus, qui moins y ont contribué leur industrie, & que par consequent il est tres raisonnable que tout plain de braues gens qui honnorent ceste profession participent à ceste loüange, sinon à pareil degré d'honneur que les premiers, au moins à mesure que chacun a de la vertu: ce qui sera d'autant plus equitable qu'ils ont acquis dequoy se faire imiter & se distinguer d'auec ceux qu'on sçait profaner le mestier.

Icy il importe que ie gauchisse encores vn peu mon chemin, pour faire veoir que cest abus est suiui d'vn autre bien plus insupportable: C'est que comme en toutes sortes de sciences il se rencontre des personnes qui pour y estre montees seulement par la fenestre, n'esperent rien moins que les mesmes priuileges de ceux qui en ont recherché l'entree par les voyes legitimes, l'on voit de mesmes en celle cy vn tas de Maistres dont les vns s'imaginent que pour rendre leurs imperfectiõs inuisibles, c'est assez de se mettre à couuert soubs les aisles de ceste belle qualité, qu'ils font le sejour de leur reputation, aussi plaisans que celuy qui couuroit son Asne de la peau du Lyon, croyant luy faire changer de nature.

Les autres sont si fort esclaues de la vanité qu'ils font gloire de professer l'ignorance, mais auec telle superstition qu'ils condamnent souuent ce qu'ils n'entendent pas, & lors qu'on choque leurs vieilles maximes, & les actions corrompuës & abastardies dont ils se

the former, at least to the measure which each has from his own faculty. This would be much more just, since they have acquired thereby the right to be imitated, and to distinguish themselves from those whom one knows profane the profession.

Here it signifies that I digress again somewhat from my course in order to make it understood that this abuse is followed by another even more insufferable, which is that, as in all kinds of sciences, some persons are met with who have entered only by the window, expecting nothing less than the same privileges as those who have sought entry by legitimate means. One sees this likewise in many Masters, of whom some imagine that in order to render their imperfections invisible, it is enough to shelter themselves beneath the wings of that good quality which they make the abode of their reputation, thus being as ludicrous as he who would cover his Ass with the skin of a Lion, thinking thereby to make him change his nature.

Others are so greatly enslaved by vanity that they glory in professing their ignorance, but with such credulity that they often condemn that which they do not understand. When one shocks their old maxims, and the corrupt and degenerate actions which they use, they estimate that it suffices to call, as a guarantee, the authority of the Masters under whom they have served their apprenticeship, thinking thereby to gain sufficient merit to eat of the marrow of Fame without considering that they have not teeth tested for gnawing the bones. Thus stupidity never lacks either prey or practice.

Now if there be some amidst these who, during the practice of their steps, have never forgotten the way of reason, I beg them to reflect a little on themselves, and to give some hours of their leisure to the unfeigned knowledge of that of which they are either capable or incapable, in order that through the practice of so profitable a study they

seruent, estiment qu'il suffit d'appeller à garand l'authorité des Maistres soubs lesquels ils ont faict leur apprentissage, & par là meriter assez pour manger la moüelle de la renommee, sans considerer qu'ils n'ont pas les dents à l'espreuue pour en ronger les os, & ainsi la sottise ne manque iamais de proye ny d'exercice.

Or s'il y en a quelques vns parmi ceux-cy qui n'ayēt pas du tout oublié par l'vsage des pas celuy de la raison, ie les coniure de faire vne petite reflection sur eux mesmes, & de donner quelques heures de leur loisir à la cognoissance non affectee de ce qu'ils sont capables ou incapables, afin que par la prattique d'vne stude si profitable, ils anoblissent ce qu'ils peuuent desia, corrigent leurs deffauts, & acquierent en fin les perfections qui rendent à bon droict imitables ceux qui les possedent, lesquelles (s'ils ne les recherchent ailleurs que dans la presomption) on trouueroit aussi tost en eux, qu'en la Sphere le rencontre de deux parallelles.

Quand à ceux qui n'ont l'esprit qu'au bout des pieds, ils ne peuuent pas auoir les considerations releuees iusques où ie les voudrois, pour leur faire trouuer quelque goust en ces aduis, ils sont trop ahurtez à la bonne opinion qu'ils ont d'eux mesmes, qu'ils s'y tiennent donc tant qu'il leur plaira, & qu'ils exercent à souhait leur iugement terre à terre, ie ne leur enuieray iamais la gloire qu'ils en rapporteront, il suffit que i'aye rendu ce tesmoignage du ressentiment qu'vne consideration publique me donne de ce qu'ils sont tels, & du contentement que i'aurois pour la mesme raison qu'ils fussent dignes d'vne recommandation veritable.

Que si ie ne m'arreste point à particulariser tant de mauuaises actions, qui feroient peut estre remarquer les personnes où elles sont, (comme certains accidents

An APOLOGY for the DANCE

may enhance that which they already are able to do, correcting their defects, and acquiring at length the perfections which rightly render those who possess them as a pattern to be imitated; which, if not sought for elsewhere than in self-conceit, would as soon be found in them as the meeting of two parallels in a Sphere.

As for those whose only intelligence is in the tips of their toes, they cannot have as exalted considerations as I would wish them in order to make them find relish in this advice. They are too bemused by the good opinion that they have of themselves. Let them then hold to these therefore as long as they wish, and if they exert their low judgment sufficiently, I shall never envy them the fame which they will bring themselves. It suffices that I shall have rendered evidence of the sentiment which public motive gives me, such as it is. Also of the happiness that I shall have for the same reason, that they were worthy of a true approbation.

How, if I do not stop to particularise many of the bad actions which make people noticeable and to which they are inseparably joined (as in certain accidents to their persons), will they know that I am in this driven by courtesy and from a sworn aversion to slanders, and not from any fear that I have, either of the effects or of the words of people who could only make me pity them? Besides, if I went deeper in this matter I would abuse the patience of everyone, and would employ my labour uselessly in the cure of an evil which might appear to have no remedy. Finally, what matters most to me is that I would leave my subject too long, the which calls me and wishes me to conclude.

This I shall do with the astonishment which has often surprised my mind. Why so many sciences, I will say not only useless but harmful, have had a vogue among people, whereas this one, which attracts the graces to itself, has been so much neglected that not one of those who make a

en leurs subiects) inseparablement coniointes, qu'on sçache que ie suis en cela poussé de courtoisie, & de mon inclination ennemie iuree de la mesdisance, & non d'aucune crainte que i'aye, ny des effects ny des paroles des gens qui ne me pourroient rien faire que pitié. D'ailleurs si ie m'enfonçois en ceste matiere, i'abuserois trop long temps de la patience du monde, & engagerois inutilement ma peine à la guerison d'vn mal qui paroist sans remede, & en fin ce qui me touche le plus, seroit abandonner de trop loing mon subiet qui me rappelle & veut que ie le concluë.

Ce que ie feray auec cest estonnement dont mon ame a souuent esté surprise. Pourquoy tant de sciĕces, ie ne diray pas seulement inutiles, mais dommageables ont eu la vogue parmi le monde, & que celle cy qui meine quand & soy les graces a tant esté disgratiee que pas vn de ceux qui en font profession, n'a laissé à la memoire le moyen qu'il falloit obseruer en sa pratique: Certes si l'on considere en cela la negligence des siecles passez, on les trouuera en quelque façon excusables eu esgard à leur insuffisance, mais au nostre où la Danse se peut venter du dernier poinct de sa perfection. N'est-ce pas vne honte que nous voulions enseuelir la gloire qu'il merite de l'y auoir amenee, & priuer la posterité d'vn bien qui nous donne vn si grand auantage sur les anciens: car comme toutes choses par vne vicissitude & reuolution presque ineuitable retournent à leur commencement, qui doute que cest exercice s'alterant auec le temps ne rentre bien tost au neant dont nous l'auons tiré, s'il ne rencontre quelque plume charitable qui luy entretienne la vie malgré l'enuie.

Mais le moyen, me dira quelqu'vn d'exprimer par escrit ce dont l'intelligence gist au voir faire? Comme si l'on n'auoit iamais escrit de choses plus difficiles à

profession of it has left to memory the means by which it may be practised. Certainly, if one considers in this the negligence of past centuries, one will find some excuse for them as regards their insufficiency. But as to our century, where the Dance can boast of a high degree of perfection, is it not shameful that we should wish to bury the glory which it deserves for having brought [the dance] so far, and to deprive posterity of a benefit which gives us such a great advantage over the ancients? For as all things by vicissitude and revolution almost always return to their beginning, who doubts that this exercise, altering with time, will return very soon to the abyss from which we have drawn it, unless it finds some charitable pen which will maintain its life in spite of that inclination?

But in what way, some will ask me, shall we express in writing that which the intelligence desires to see done? As though one had never written of things more difficult to understand! A Philosopher said to me one day, that just as words were the tokens of the ideas of our soul, writings were also the reflections of words. For things beget themselves words in order to communicate themselves to those present, and from words come writings. But in consideration for the past, and for posterity, that which is not the office of words he taught me by examples and such palpable reasonings that a man with common sense cannot doubt it —that when the intellect has fully understood the knowledge of the things which come to it, through the mediation of the senses, it can happily be clarified by the means of one or the other of the two instruments of which I have just spoken. This has so strengthened my opinion in that which I had already gained through experience, that I make bold to maintain that whomsoever has the imagination full of one science or another can make himself understood either through speech or in writing, if not to all, at least to those of his profession. I admit that the Dance has something

comprendre? Vn Philosophe me dit vn iour, que cõme les paroles estoiẽt les marques des cõceptiõs de nostre ame, les escrits estoient aussi les images des paroles, que des choses s'enfantoiẽt les paroles pour les communiquer aux presens, & des paroles les escrits, mais en consideration des absens & de nos posterieurs, ce qui n'est pas l'office des paroles, il m'apprit encores par des exemples & des raisons si palpables, qu'vn homme auec du sens commun n'en peut douter, que lors que l'intellect a bien compris la cognoissance des choses qui luy arriue par l'entremise des sens, il la peut heureusement esclarcir par le moyen de l'vn ou l'autre de ces deux instruments dont ie viens de parler, cela m'a tellement fortifié en l'opinion que i'en auois desia par experience, que i'ose maintenir, que quiconque a l'imagination plaine de quelque science, il se peut faire entendre ou de voix ou d'escrit, sinon à tous, pour le moins à ceux de sa profession. I'auouë bien que la danse a quelque chose de particulier qui l'annoblit & l'anime, comme vn certain air, ou vn maintien tantost graue, & tantost negligent qu'vne plume ne peut apprendre, mais qu'outre les pas on ne puisse encores enseigner les actions plus necessaires, qui donnent vn facile acheminement à ceste perfection, qui consiste à voir faire vn bon Maistre, sont des impossibilitez que ie feray voir imaginaires en ce traicté, duquel non seulement plusieurs qui se meslent d'enseigner, mais les Escoliers mesme peuuent tirer vn grand soulagement.

particular which ennobles and animates it, such as a certain air, or a bearing sometimes sedate and sometimes negligent, which the pen cannot teach, but [to say] that beyond the steps one is unable further to teach the more necessary actions, which give an easy progress towards this perfection, and that it consists in seeing a good Master demonstrate, are difficulties which I shall show in this Treatise to be imaginary, from which not only many who profess to teach, but Scholars themselves, may derive great benefits.

METHODE POVR LES CAVALIERS

C'EVX qui croyent l'obseruation de plusieurs figures du tout necessaires pour biē monstrer à danser par liure, & representer plus naïuemēt les mouuemens qui se doiuent obseruer à la danse, ne s'accordent pas mal auec cest Orateur, qui ayant iadis à haranguer en plain Senat sur vn faict tres-attroce, commit ceste lourde faute d'en proposer vn tableau deuant les yeux des Iuges, se fiant plus aux traits muets d'vne morte peinture qu'à l'energie d'vne eloquence viue. Ie laisse aux partisans de ce digne Orateur, (qui auront quelque dessein de s'opposer à la ruyne de cest exercice) l'vsage de telles inuentions, il me suffit que ma plume les face voir inutiles au subiect que i'ay pris, & dont il est temps que ie parle. Mais à cause qu'il y a de la difference entre les pas & les actions d'vn Caualier, & ce qu'il faut qu'vne Dame face : & aussi qu'il y auroit de la confusion d'instruire l'vn & l'autre ensemble, il m'a semblé bon de commencer par le Caualier, auquel ie conseillerois volontiers qu'il n'attendit pas à vn aage trop aduancé, pource qu'estant alors moins maniable, il aura plus de difficulté à s'aquerir la perfection qui luy seroit aisee à vn temps plus commode ; ce bon-heur neanmoins se peut recouurer par vne peine volontaire, qu'vn enfant manque de discretion ne peut auoir, toutesfois pource qu'il y a de certaines actions plaines de graces, qu'il est impossible d'escrire, (comme il me souuient d'auoir dit en quelque lieu) qu'il se garde bien de se mettre entre les mains d'vn ignorant, ny mesme s'il est possible, de celuy qui outre l'excellence de sa methode, ne sçache encore executer

THE METHOD FOR GENTLEMEN

THOSE who believe that to teach dancing properly from a book necessitates numerous illustrations, in order to describe more plainly the movements which should be observed in dancing, are in agreement with that Orator of old, who, having to harangue in open Senate on an atrocious deed, committed this clumsy fault of setting up a painting before the eyes of the Judges, trusting more in the dumb strokes of a dead painting, than to the energy of living eloquence. I leave to the partisans of this worthy Orator, who may have some intention to set themselves to ruin this exercise, the practise of such inventions. It suffices me that my pen will make them seem unnecessary to the subject which I have undertaken and of which it is time that I spoke. But because there is a difference between the steps and actions of a Gentleman and those which a Lady must make, and also that there would be some confusion by instructing both together, it has seemed good to me to begin with the Gentleman, to whom I would readily advise that he does not wait till a too advanced age. For, being then less tractable, he would have more difficulty in acquiring the perfection which would be easy to him at a more favourable time. This felicity he may regain, nevertheless, with willing effort, which a child, from lack of discretion, cannot have. Always providing that he has a certain grace of movement which is impossible to write of, as I recollect having said elsewhere. Let him have a care of putting himself into the hands of an ignoramus, neither, if it is possible, into the hands of he who, apart from the excellence of his method, is not able to execute what is beyond speech and writing. For, without knowledge one is unable to judge of a

ce qui est par dessus la voix & l'escriture: car l'vn ne pourra iuger d'vne belle actiõ ne la cognoissant pas, moins encore la remettre en son entier si elle est corrompuë, & quelque habile homme que soit l'autre, il se tourmenteroit en vain sur l'intelligence d'vne chose qui conciste plus en vsage qu'en artifice; si mes actions doiuent prendre loy de celles de mon Maistre, & qu'il ne sçache effectuer ce qu'il veut que ie face, i'aymerois autant qu'on me fit ioüer le personnage d'vne Idole; c'est vne maxime trop aueree, qu'en cecy la Pratique & la Theorie doiuent estre deux accidens inseparables.

DES PRINCIPES DE LA DANSE

C*ELVY donc qui aura ces qualitez & qui fera profession de les communiquer, doit premierement apprendre à cheminer à son escolier, car quelque gentillesse qu'il ait naturellement, il ne le peut auec la iustesse requise, soit pour l'action de la veuë, port de la iambe, ou grauité des demarches, qui se doiuent faire en droite ligne, sans plier le genoüil, la pointe des pieds ouuerte en sorte que les mouuemens francs de toute timidité procedent de la hanche.*

Ceste façon de cheminer toute graue & noble, luy apportera auec vne grande facilité à la danse, vn maintien plus asseuré pour aborder, ou receuoir de bonne grace quelque compagnie, ce que luy estant impossible de soy qu'on luy face pratiquer l'instruction que i'en donne.

The METHOD for GENTLEMEN

beautiful movement, even less to restore it wholly if it is spoiled, and however skilful the other man is, he would torment himself in vain in the understanding of a thing which is obtained more by practice than by cunning. If my actions should take as a pattern those of my Master, and if he knows not how to perform that which he wishes me to do, I would as much like to be made to play the part of an Idol. It is a well-proved maxim that in this, Practice and Theory should be two inseparable contingencies.

ON THE PRINCIPLES OF THE DANCE

HE then who has these qualities, and who will profess to communicate them, should firstly teach his scholar how to walk. For, whatever gentility he would have naturally, he would be unable to do this of himself with the required exactness, whether for the movement of the eyes, the carriage of the leg, or the gravity of his steps, which should be made in a straight line, without bending the knee, the toes well outwards, in a manner that the movements, free from all timidity, proceed from the hip.

This manner of walking, wholly grave and noble, will bring to him great ease in dancing, an assured bearing in approaching, or receiving, with good grace any company, but which, of himself, would be impossible unless he be made to practise the instructions which I give here.

ON THE BOW

AFTER having removed the hat with the right hand, which he will hold negligently—not on the thigh as was formerly the custom, but in front of the busk of the pourpoint—by the left hand in order to leave the other free, he

METHODE *povr les* CAVALIERS

DE LA REVERENCE

APRES *auoir tiré le chapeau de la main droite qu'il portera negligemment, non sur la cuisse comme on souloit faire, ains deuant le busque du pourpoint sur la main gauche pour laisser l'autre libre, regardant d'vn visage riant la compagnie, qu'il s'aduance, mais auec des demarches graues & sans contrainte, & lors que sa discretion luy fera iuger le temps de faire la reuerance, sans plier les genoux, qu'il coule doucement la iambe droite deuant iusque à ce qu'elle touche quasi la gauche, & sans s'arrester que bien peu la dessus, la pointe des pieds fort ouuertes en pliant doucement l'vne & l'autre, il desgagera comme insensiblement la gauche, & continuëra ainsi iusqu'à ce qu'il ait ioint ceux qui l'y obligent, que s'il se trouuoit, comme il est ordinaire, plusieurs compagnies en vn mesme lieu, il fera ces mesmes reuerences sur l'vn & sur l'autre pied, selon que les personnes seront placées, toutesfois sans aucun geste ou posture du corps: car en cela la seule conduite de la veue est suffisante.*

Il y a encores deux ou trois autres sortes de reuerences, comme pour saluer vn Seigneur, vne Dame; commencer vne courante, ou vne gaillarde, desquelles ie discourray en leur lieu; Mais parce que les pas de courante sont tres-propres pour aquerir la liberté des mouuemens qui sont necessaires en la danse, & adoucir l'air à vn Cauallier, & aussi que l'exercisse d'iceux fait trouuer de la facillité aux autres danses, ie commenceray par la.

The METHOD *for* GENTLEMEN

advances towards the company, looking at them with a smiling countenance, all be it with slow steps, without awkwardness. And when his discretion makes him judge the moment to make his bow, without bending his knees, he gently slides the right leg in front till [in passing] it nearly touches the left. Then, without stopping thereupon, except but a little, in gently bending both knees, the toes well turned out, he will disengage the left, as it were, insensibly, and will thus continue until he has joined those to whom he is indebted. Then if he finds, as is usual, several assemblies in the same place, he will make these same bows, on one foot or the other, according as to how the people are placed, always without any gesture or posture of the body; because in this the direction of the eyes is sufficient.

There are besides two or three other kinds of bows, like that for saluting a Lord, a Lady, beginning a *Courante* or a *Gaillarde*, of which I will discourse in their place. But because the steps of the *Courante* are very proper for acquiring the freedom of the movements which are necessary in the dance, and soften the style of a Gentleman, and also that the practice of these will be found to make the other dances easier, I will begin with this.

ON THE COURANTE IN GENERAL

IF it be someone who has never learnt to dance, it will be very advantageous to make him lean with his hands against a table, in order to give him greater ease in learning the movements which are necessary, as much for the knee and the hip as for the foot. And having placed him as is required to begin a *Courante*, one must make him carry his leg in front and behind, sometimes in a straight line, and sometimes over and under the leg which is on the ground, to make him learn the connections. Hence, all the move-

DE LA COVRANTE EN GENERAL

SY c'est quelqu'vn qui n'aye iamais apris à danser sera fort bon de le faire apuyer des mains contre vne table, pour luy donner plus de facilité à aprendre les mouuemens qui sont necessaires, tant du genoüil, & de la hanche, que du pied, & l'ayant fait placer comme il est requis d'estre pour commencer vne courante, faut luy faire porter la iambe en auãt & en arriere, tantost en droicte ligne, & quelque fois dessus & dessous la iambe qui sera à terre, pour luy apprendre les liaisons, le tout sans mettre à terre que pour se soulager ou pour changer de iambe, afin de faire de mesme de l'autre, dont tous les mouuemens procedent de la hanche, la pointe tant du pied qui sera en l'air que de celuy qui sera à terre fort ouuertes, & par ce que cela luy acquerra insensiblement la facilité de bien passer la capriolle, & l'entrechart, s'il a le corps disposé à la danse par haut, il luy faut souuent faire exercer ceste leçon: Apres laquelle afin de luy acquerir auec moins de peine le port de la iambe, qu'on luy face sans le desplacer plier esgalement les deux genoux pour prendre le tẽps du pas de courante, mais parce que toutes les cadances se doiuent marquer en l'air: Venant à s'esleuer faut prendre garde que le pied qui se trouuera derriere demeure en l'air, & ne passe le talon de celuy de deuant, & que celuy de deuant ne leue qu'apres celuy de derriere, & le faire tomber tousiours sur la pointe du pied, & quand on l'aura ainsi exercé sur l'vne & sur l'autre iambe, qu'on luy face former le pas entier, & vn pas chassé sans appuy, tant en auant qu'en arriere & de costé, sur lesquels on l'asseurera auant que luy faire entreprendre ce qui suit.

The METHOD for GENTLEMEN

ments proceeding from the hip, the toe of the foot which will be in the air, as well as that on the ground, will be well turned out, and inasmuch as this will enable him to acquire insensibly the ease of crossing well in the *capriole* and the *entrechat*, if he has a good figure for dancing high he must be made to practise this lesson frequently. After which, in order to make him acquire the movement of the leg with the least trouble, that he be made, without changing place, to bend both knees equally so as to take the *temps* of the *pas de Courante*. But because all the cadences should be marked in the air, when rising one must take care that the foot which is behind remains in the air, and does not pass the heel of the one in front, and that that of the front only rises after that of the back, and make it fall always on to the toe. And when one shall have practised thus, on one leg and the other, then one can make him form the complete step, and a *pas chassé* without support, as well forwards as backwards and to the side, of which one will make him certain before one makes him undertake that which follows.

ON THE COURANTE

WITHOUT holding therefore to the ancient maxims of the times when one could truly say, "those who dance always progress", which were as far removed from the perfection of which the dance is glorified today, as they were destitute of the nicety of the actions and movements of the body, together with the delicacy of the steps whereof it is [now] enriched. It is necessary that a scholar should seek with diligence the means which can conquer the difficulties which prevent him from acquiring the graces, and that he should consider that if the rose cannot be gathered except among thorns, one also only acquires this exercise by the exercise itself. Then when the scholar will be

DE LA COVRANTE

*S*ANS *s'attacher donc aux vieilles maximes du temps, où l'on pouuoit veritablement dire, tousiours va qui danse, qui estoient autant esloignees de la perfection dont la danse se glorifie à ceste heure, comme elles estoient destituees de la gentillesse, des actions & mouuemens du corps, ioints à la mignardise des pas dont elle est enrichie, il faut qu'vn Escolier recherche curieusement les moyens qui peuuent vaincre les difficultez qui s'opposent à receuoir ses graces, & qu'il considere, que si la rose ne se peut cueillir que parmy les espines : aussi ne gagne-on cest exercice que par l'exercice mesme. Lors donc que l'Escolier fera facilement ce qui a esté dit cy dessus, il luy faudra apprendre vne courante reglee des plus aisees, comme celle qui suit, de laquelle ie parleray, afin de monstrer seulement quels y doiuent estre les mouuemens du corps, & comme il y faut porter & asseoir les pas : mais parce qu'elle se commence par vne reuerence, ie diray la methode qu'il faut tenir pour la bien faire.*

DE LA REVERENCE, AVANT COMMENCER VNE COVRANTE

*A*YANT *tiré le chapeau de la main gauche deuant la compagnie & iceluy porté negligemment sur la cuisse, sans baisser la teste, tenant tousiours la veuë esgalle de sa hauteur, faut apres auoir tant soit peu plié les genoux, faire porter du pied droict vn pas plus en arriere qu'à costé, la iambe bien tenduë, puis en pliant à loisir le genoüil de l'autre, la faire suiure quasi derriere sur le mouuement du pied, & à l'instant sans se forcer, glisser l'autre par dessus, & lors que*

The METHOD for GENTLEMEN

familiar with that which has been said above, it is necessary to make him learn one of the easiest *Courante Reglée*, such as that which follows, of which I shall speak merely in order to show what the movements of the body ought to be, and how one must dispose and set the steps. But because it begins with a bow, I will state the best method of doing this.

ON THE BOW BEFORE BEGINNING THE COURANTE

HAVING removed the hat before the company with the left hand, and carried it negligently on the thigh, without lowering the head, always keeping the eyes at their own level, one must, after having bent the knees a little, make a step with the right foot more to the back than to the side, the leg well stretched. Then, bending at leisure the knee of the other, make it follow almost behind on the ball of the foot, and at that instant, without forcing it, slide the other over it; and when the calves of the legs come together, without pausing but a little on this action, make both knees bend with equal smoothness. And in disengaging, as it were insensibly, the left leg, the toe raised, turn facing the side where the lady ought to be, in order to make the same bow with the other foot. Then lowering the head slightly with the body, one must kiss one's hand to take that of the lady, and putting on one's hat begin gaily [to dance] in observing a rather quick measure. When the scholar will be familiar with that which follows, I intend that then, and not before, one must show the manner which should be observed to take out a Lady and to ask her to dance, of which I will speak hereafter in the *Gaillarde*.

les molets des iambes viendront à se ioindre, sans s'arrester que bien peu sur ceste action, faire plier auec la mesme douceur les deux genoux, & en desgageant comme insensiblement la iambe gauche, la pointe du pied releuee, se tourner vis à vis, du costé où doit estre la femme, afin de faire la mesme reuerence de l'autre pied, puis baissant vn peu la teste auec le corps faut baiser la main pour prendre celle de la femme, & se couurant, commencer gayement en obseruant vne mesure vn peu viste: i'entends quand l'Escolier sera bien asseuré sur ce qui suit, auquel alors & non plustost, il faudra monstrer l'action qui doit estre obseruee pour prendre vne Dame, & la prier de danser, dont sera parlé cy apres à la gaillarde.

DE LA COVRANTE REGLEE

IL faut au partir de la reuerence, commencer du pied droict & faire trois pas, auec quelque negligence sans trainer à terre, & s'esleuant sur la pointe des pieds, les genoux tendus, tourner vn peu l'espaule en dedans, du costé du pied qui auance, puis remettant le corps à son naturel, faire vn chasse-coulant deuant soy, & selon la grandeur du lieu, faire cognoistre à l'Escolier qu'il n'importe d'auancer apres le chasse, quelques pas non pairs, comme trois ou cinq sans chasser. Apres lesquels s'arrestant sur la pointe du pied droict, luy faire porter l'autre en l'air, la iambe fort tenduë pour faire vn temps en rond, qui sera porté à costé, dont le mouuement doit proceder de la hanche pour bien former lequel, il faut vn peu plier sur l'autre iambe, & se releuer sur la pointe du pied; apres lequel temps faut faire vn chasse horsterre du mesme costé, puis sautant sur le pied gauche, faire porter

The METHOD for GENTLEMEN

ON THE COURANTE REGLÉE

ON coming out of the bow one should begin with the right foot, and make three steps, with some negligence, without dragging on the ground, but rising on to the toes, the legs stretched. Turn the shoulder on that side of the foot which advances a little inwards, then returning the body to its natural position, make a *chassé-coulant* (sliding *chassé*) in front. And according to the size of the space, make the scholar understand that it is necessary to advance after the *chassé* some uneven number of steps only, such as three or five, with no *chassé*. After which, stopping on the right toe, make him carry the other in the air, the leg well stretched, in order to make a *temps en rond* (circular step), which will be carried to the side, whereof the movement should proceed from the hip in order to be well executed. One must bend a little on the other leg and rise again on to the toe. After which *temps* one must make a *chassé* off the ground to the same side, then springing on the left foot, carry the other, the leg well stretched, not in front as some do, who by this means incommode a lady, but to the side in the air, to carry it with the same *temps* on the ground, the leg crossed in a manner that the calves touch. This *retirade* ought to be followed by another, which one makes in the same way with the other foot, and because on this action the right foot is found in front, one must carry it to the side, on which having made a *chassé* one must make two steps forward. After which the left foot should be carried in the air, without bending the knee, to make a *temps en rond* as above to the same [left] side, which ought to be accompanied with a *feinte*, by turning to the right hand in bending the knee which is on that side, and *chassé* on the other, turning to replace the body to its natural position. Then advance three steps and *chassé* forward without turning the shoulders either one way or the other, and thus continue

l'autre, la iambe bien tenduë, non en auant, comme plusieurs font, qui par ce moyen incommodent vne femme: mais à costé, en l'air, pour le porter d'vn mesme temps à terre, la iambe croisee, en sorte que les molets se touchent; Ceste retirade doit estre suiuie d'vne autre qu'on fera tout de mesme de l'autre pied, & parce que sur ceste action, le pied droict se trouue deuant, il le faut porter à costé, sur lequel ayant chassé, faut faire deux pas deuant soy, apres lesquels le pied gauche se doit porter en l'air, pour d'iceluy sans plier le genoüil faire du mesme costé vn temps en rond comme le susdit, qui doit estre accompagné d'vne feinte, de tourner sur la main droicte en pliant le genoüil qui se trouue du mesme costé, & chasser sur l'autre, en tournant pour remettre le corps à son naturel, puis auancer trois pas, & chasser deuant soy sans tourner les espaules de costé ny d'autre, & ainsi continuer encore deux pas, & au troisiesme, la iambe bien tẽduë, faire vn temps en rond semblable au premier, & apres l'auoir chassé, faire deux retirades de mesmes les deux precedentes, & vne troisiesme du pied droict sans croiser, sur laquelle au lieu d'vn chassé on peut releuer vn temps de la iambe gauche sans sauter, en s'esleuãt sur la pointe du pied droict, que le corps tout d'vne piece penchant vers la main droicte doit suiure lentement, & en mesme temps qu'on aura passe le pied gauche par dessus l'autre, faut desgager le droict, & le porter encore vne fois à costé à fin de glisser à l'instant le gauche derriere, puis faire vne retirade croisee, qui doit estre suiuie d'vne autre sans croiser, mais portee plustost en arriere qu'à costé, sur laquelle pliant le genoüil droict, faut tourner vn peu le corps de ce mesme costé, à fin de mieux prendre son temps pour faire vn chasse, & deux pas en tournant de l'autre, apres lesquels passant vne

The METHOD for GENTLEMEN

for two more steps; and on the third, with the leg well stretched, make a *temps en rond* like the first. And after making a *chassé*, make two *retirades* the same as the two preceding ones, and a third with the right foot without crossing, on which, instead of a *chassé*, one may raise the left leg for one *temps* without springing, by raising oneself on to the toe of the right foot, so that the body should follow slowly, leaning all in one piece to the right-hand [side]. And at the same time that one will have crossed the left foot over the other, one must disengage the right and carry it once more to the side, in order to slide the left behind at the same instant. Then make a crossed *retirade*, which ought to be followed by one without being crossed, but carried more to the back than to the side, on which, bending the right knee, one must turn the body a little to the same [right] side, in order to take his time (*temps*) better to make a *chassé*, and two turning steps to the other side. After which, crossing a *demi-capriole* with the right foot over the left, or making the time (*temps*) of this, take the left to the side in the air, and at the same time, rising on to the toe of the other, carry it over, the leg well stretched, in a manner that it crosses. Then, after having disengaged the left which is behind, and with it made a *temps* in turning the body to that side where one commenced, and *chassé* on it, it is only necessary to cross a *demi-capriole* in turning before the lady, or at least to take the time (*temps*) to finish a bow.

ON THE MORE NECESSARY ACTIONS WHICH SHOULD BE OBSERVED IN THE COURANTE

AND because the grace of a *Courante* depends in part on the actions of the arms, it is necessary thereafter to learn to mark the cadences by their movements. Taking them then in their natural position, one must, when bend-

❖ METHODE *pour les* CAVALIERS

demy capriolle du pied droict par dessus le gauche ou faisant le temps, d'icelle faut porter le gauche à costé en l'air, & d'vn mesme temps en s'esleuant sur la pointe de l'autre, le porter par dessus, la iambe bien tenduë, en sorte qu'elle croise, si bien qu'apres auoir desgagé la gauche qui se trouue derriere, & d'icelle faict vn temps, en tournant le corps du costé qu'on aura commencé & chassé sur iceluy, il ne faut que passer vne demy capriole en tournant deuant la femme, ou du moins en faire le temps pour finir vne reuerence.

DES ACTIONS PLVS NECESSAIRES QVI DOIVENT ESTRE OBSERVEES A LA COURANTE

ET parce que la grace d'vne Courante consiste en partie en l'action des bras, il faut par apres apprendre à marquer les cadences par le mouuement d'iceux, les prenant donc à leur naturel, faut en pliant le genoüil porter esgalemẽt les deux mains vers le busque du pourpoint, sans plier le poignet, & en se releuant pour former le premier pas, ouurir vn peu les bras, dont les mouuemens soient doux & sans force, & ainsi accompagnant de ceste action tous les pas, sans se laisser vaincre à l'impatience, il se faut bien exercer là dessus: car d'entreprendre beaucoup à la fois il est impossible de se rendre capable que de bien peu. Au contraire suiuant l'ordre que i'ay icy establi, on pourra mener aisément en peu de temps vn Escolier, au contentement qu'il en auroit imaginé: & lors que l'Escolier aura bien compris ceste courante, où telle autre qui luy sera monstree, ensemble les mouuements susdits, à fin que rien ne luy defaille, il luy faut faire obseruer aux pas chassez, qui se font en auançant ou

The METHOD for GENTLEMEN

ing the knee, carry both hands alike toward the busk of the pourpoint, without bending the wrist, and in rising again to make the first step open the arms a little, of which the movements should be gentle and not forced; and thus accompany all the steps with this action, without allowing oneself to be conquered by impatience. It is necessary to practise the above often, for by undertaking too much at a time it is only possible to render oneself capable of a little. On the contrary, by following the order which I have set forth here, one may easily lead a scholar to his satisfaction in a very little time. And when the scholar will have thoroughly understood this *Courante*, or any other which will be shown him, unite the above movements. So that nothing will be omitted, one must make him observe that in the *pas chassés*, which are made in advancing or retiring, he should carry the foot which makes the *chassé* to the side of the one which is overtaken; not behind as some do who, in so doing, push forward their stomachs. In the *chassés* which are made to the side, the foot which makes the *chassé* must take the place of that which is overtaken: and in putting the first on the ground on the ball, the other is placed first on the heel, and is made in a manner that the body is held erect from the busk to the eyes, which are always at their own level, without bending from the waist, the knees never inwards. Neither shake the head, but do it so that the body, held firm and erect, always accompanies the actions of the feet, principally in the *retirades* where some sway the body, either through affectation or bad habit.

The aforesaid *Courante* well executed, with the required measure and with such actions that have here been described, will give great ease to all other kinds of dances, and from this time on the scholar will begin to take pleasure therein. He will perceive how, with patience, time will bring him insensibly this familiar knowledge, which at last renders easy to him all that which before seemed impossible.

reculant, à porter le pied qui chasse au costé du chassé, non derriere, comme il y en a qui font, qui en ce faisant auancent le ventre; & aux chassez qui se font de costé, faut que le pied qui chasse prenne la place du chassé, & que le portant le premier à terre sur le mouuement, l'autre soit assis d'abord sur le talon, & faire en sorte qu'il y tienne le corps droict, depuis le busque iusques aux yeux, & la veuë tousiours esgale de sa hauteur, sans plier de la ceincture, ny iamais les genoux en dedans, pas mesmes bransler la teste, mais faire que le corps ferme & droict accompagne tousiours l'action des pieds aux retirades principalement, ou plusieurs balancent le corps, soit par affecterie ou mauuaise habitude.

La susdite Courante bien executee, auec la mesure requise, & auec les actions telles qu'elles y sont depeintes, donnera vne grande facilité à toute autre sorte de danses, & dés l'heure l'Escolier commençant à y prendre plaisir, s'apperceura comme auec la patience, le temps luy amene insensiblement ceste familiere cognoissance, qui luy rend en fin doux tout ce qui luy sembloit auparauant impossible, & sans qu'il soit besoin de plus ample instruction, les Maistres pourront par le moyen de la Courante & actions susdites en composer tout autant d'autres qu'il leur plairra, pourueu qu'ils n'ignorent la valeur des temps, & autres pas, & mouuemens dont on les enrichit, & qu'on danse auiourd'huy, d'vne certaine negligence nullement affectee; & n'aymerois point qu'ils meslassent parmy leurs compositions des pas qui sentissent son baladin, comme fleurets, frisoteries, ou branslemens de pieds, piroüetes (i'entens à plusieurs tours violens & forcez,) caprioles, pas mesmes des demy caprioles, si ce n'est en tournant ou finissant, & tout plain d'autres petites actions ennemies du vray air

The METHOD for GENTLEMEN

And without it being necessary for more ample instruction, Masters will be able, by the means of the aforesaid *Courante* and actions, to compose as many others as they please, provided that they do not ignore the value of the *temps* and other steps and movements whereof one enriches them. Also that people dance today with a certain unaffected negligence, and no longer like to mix among their compositions steps which look like those of a juggler, such as *fleurets*, *frisoteries*, or shakings of the feet; *pirouettes* (I mean several violent and forced turns), *caprioles*, nor even *demi-caprioles* if it be not in turning or finishing. Even of all the other little actions [which are] antagonistic to the true manner which one should observe. But only those of the *pas coupez* and *entre-coupez*, otherwise sedate steps, together with *liaisons* (connecting steps), and some elegant *temps*, because the movements which proceed from these can, with sufficient air and grace, accompany such steps without effort. And if some people are offended by this advice, and failing to become known, vanity causes them to consider vain the trouble which I take, let them know that charity alone has been my object: Since truth and reason are common to all, they neither belong to he who speaks first, nor to he who speaks last, and thus, without departing from the truth, let them do better if they can.

ON THE BRANSLES

IT is quite time, now that the scholar may have acquired the carriage of the leg, to show him the *Suite of Bransles*. For as much as by these one may make him greatly soften his style, and regulate the action of the body and of the eyes, which one could not have done previously with so much ease. Not that they are blameworthy who, to avoid wearying or displeasing a scholar, make him begin with

qu'on y doit obseruer, mais seulement des pas coupez, & entrecoupez, d'autres graues, ensemble des liaisons, & des beaux temps, parce que les mouuemens qui en procedent, peuuent auec assez d'air & de grace accompagner tels pas sans force; que si quelques vns d'eux s'offencẽt de c'est aduis & que manque de se sçauoir cognoistre, la vanité leur face iuger vaine la peine que ie prends, qu'ils apprennent que la charité seule m'en a serui d'obiect: loint que la verité & la raison estans communes à vn chacun ne sont non plus à qui les a dictes premierement, qu'à celuy qui les dict apres, & ainsi sans s'en esloigner, qu'ils facent meux s'ils peuuent.

DES BRANSLES

IL est fort à propos maintenant qu'vn Escolier peut auoir acquis le port de la iambe, de luy monstrer la suitte des Bransles, d'autant que par iceux on luy pourra grandement adoucir l'air, & luy regler l'action du corps & de la veuë, ce qu'on n'eust peu auparauant auec tant de facilité, non que ceux là soient blasmables, qui pour n'ennuyer ou desgouter vn Escolier, luy font commencer iceux durant le tẽps qu'il s'exerce sur ce qui a esté dit cy deuant: Pourueu toutesfois qu'ils preuiennent l'inconuenient, que l'embrasser trop de leçons à la fois apporte. Le plus court chemin n'est pas tousiours le meilleur, principalement en cest exercice, où il n'en prend pas comme iadis à ces Abderites *qui deuiendrent Tragediens pour auoir ouy seulement reciter l'Andromede d'Euripide: Ie veux dire, que quelque suffisance que celuy qui guide vn Escolier puisse auoir, son eloquence sera sans fruict, pour luy donner l'intelligence de son vtilité, si quant &*

The METHOD for GENTLEMEN

these during that time when he should practise that which has been said above; always providing that they foresee the difficulties which encompass too many lessons at a time. The shortest road is not always the best, especially in this exercise, where it is not applicable, as in olden days, to those Abderites who would become Tragedians by having, indeed, only recited the Andromeda of Euripides. I wish to say that whatever capacity he who guides a scholar may have, his eloquence will be fruitless to give the intelligence of its use, if neither the master nor the scholar takes the time and the trouble which are necessary to enable him to acquire it worthily. For it often happens to those, who through contempt pass lightly over, that there arise occasions when they find themselves scorned, not knowing, as one says, on which foot to dance.

ON THE BOW BEFORE BEGINNING THE BRANSLES

SO as not to pervert this order [the *Bransle*] will be commenced with a Bow, which should be made as has been said in the *Courante*. In the event of dancing before a King, or whether in the presence of any persons of quality, or else in turning before the lady, it should begin with the left foot, with which, without bending the knees, having the toes outwards, one must take a step to the side and make the right foot follow almost behind. Then slide the other over it until the legs come together, and on this movement pause a little; then, gently bending both knees, raise the toe of the right foot, disengaging it gently, kissing his hand in order to take that of the lady. And putting on his hat, place himself in order to begin.

quant & l'vn l'autre n'employent le temps & la peine qui sont necessaires pour s'en pouuoir acquiter dignement, car il arriue souuent à ceux qui par mespris passent legerement par dessus, qu'estans aux occasions ils s'y trouuent eux mesmes mesprisez, ne sçachans (comme on dit) sur quel pied danser.

DE LA REVERENCE AVANT COMMENCER LES BRANSLES

POVR ne peruertir donc l'ordre, il sera commence par vne Reuerence, laquelle se doit faire comms il a esté dict à la Courante, en cas qu'on dansaté deuant vn Roy, où en la presence de quelques personnes qualifiees, sinon se tournant deuant la femme, elle se doit commencer du pied gauche, duquel sans plier les genoux, ayant les pointes ouuertes, faut porter vn pas à costé, & faire suiure le droict quasi derriere, puis glisser l'autre par dessus, iusqu'à ce que les iambes viennent à se ioindre, & sur ceste action s'arrester tant soit peu, puis pliant doucement les deux genoux & releuant la pointe du pied droict, le desgager doucement, en baisant la main pour prendre celle de la femme, & se couurant, se remettre à fin de commencer.

DV PREMIER BRANSLE

AV sortir de la Reuerence, tenant le corps bien droict, faut partir du pied gauche, qu'on portera à costé, & faire que d'iceluy on marque tousiours le tour circulaire du lieu, ce qui sera bien aisé en faisant tenir la pointe du pied fort ouuerte. Le deuxiesme

The METHOD *for* GENTLEMEN

ON THE FIRST BRANSLE

AT the end of the Bow, holding the body very erect, one must set off with the left foot, which one carries to the side, describing with it always a circular step on the spot, which will be quite easy in holding the toe well outwards. The second step should slide, stiffening the leg, until the heel comes almost to the toe of the first step. To make the third, one must disengage the left foot, and carry it level with the other, the distance of half a foot only; and upon that, rising on to the toes, gently join the right heel to the left, without bending the knees. Then separate the left to the side a half-foot or thereabouts, and slide the right foot across behind on the toe, in order to slide the left gently to the side, making it take a "round" towards the heel of the other, to carry it level and apart as the first. And finish with the right foot by a *pas glissé*, which will be placed by the toe of the left, quite flat on the ground, like that of the second, the other remaining on the toe to repeat the same steps. Thus continue the *Bransle*, in which it should be observed that one need only count eight steps, to give greater ease to a scholar; the three first of which ought to be made quite flat on the ground, the others on the ball of the foot, except the last, as has been said. Take care that the scholar holds his body as in the movement of the first step, and when putting it to the ground, that the [last step with the] right foot be straightway on the toe, so that the leg, being greatly stretched, follows it easily.

And forasmuch as some, whether from constraint or bad habit, hardly ever divert their eyes while dancing this *Bransle*, thus always looking fixedly before them at the same object, it seems to the purpose to remark that, when making the first step, one also turns the eyes modestly, at the level of one's own height, to the side. And on the third and fourth [steps] look to the front, and because the sixth slides

pas se doit glisser en roidissant la iambe, iusqu'à ce que le talon paruienne quasi à la pointe du premier pas, pour faire le troisiesme, faut desgager le pied gauche & le porter esgal à l'autre, esloigné de demy pied seulement, & là dessus en s'esleuant sur la pointe des pieds, assembler doucement (sans plier les genoux) le talon droict au gauche, puis escarter à costé le gauche d'vn demy pied ou enuiron, & glisser le pied droict derriere en croix sur la pointe, à fin de couler doucement le gauche à costé, en luy faisant prendre vn tour vers le talon de l'autre, pour le porter esgal & esloigné comme le premier, & finir du pied droict par vn pas glissé, qui sera assis à la pointe du gauche tout plat à terre, semblable au second, l'autre demeurant sur la pointe pour recommencer les mesmes pas, & ainsi continuer le bransle, auquel faut obseruer qu'il ne faut compter que huict pas, pour donner plus de facilité à vn Escolier, les trois premiers desquels se doiuent porter tous plats à terre, les autres sur le mouuement du pied, excepté le dernier, comme il a esté dit, & prendre garde que l'Escolier porte le corps quant & quant l'action du premier pas, & qu'en le posant à terre, le pied droict soit aussi tost sur la pointe, pour le faire suiure doucement, la iambe fort tenduë.

Et d'autant que plusieurs, soit par contrainte, où par mauuaise habitude ne diuertissent quasi iamais leur veuë en dansant ce bransle, ains regardent tousiours fixement deuant eux vn mesme obiect, il m'a semblé à propos de faire obseruer, qu'en portant le premier pas, on face aussi porter modestement de ce costé la veuë de sa hauteur, & au trois & quatriesme, regarder en presence, & parce que le sixiesme se glisse derriere & oblige le corps à tourner tant soit peu du costé droict, il est bon que la veuë l'accompagne auec

The METHOD for GENTLEMEN

behind and obliges the body to turn a little to the right side, it is well that the eyes should accompany it, with some negligence, without moving the head; for such movements only ennoble the other parts of the dance.

ON THE SECOND BRANSLE

THE second is named the *Bransle Gay*, which is composed of four steps, and in order to get the cadence better begins with the last [of these], by bending the knees a little so as to join both heels in rising on to the toes. Then, to begin the four steps, one must set aside the left foot, and make the other follow it, close up against the heel on the ball of the foot; and in raising the toe of the left foot, let it go gently to the side, in sliding on the heel, during which *pas glissé* one must lower the heel of the right foot flat on the ground. Without stopping there, the knees must be bent a very little so as to join the right foot to the left while rising on to the toes of both feet to begin again. Then, when one knows how to do this *Bransle*, and not before, to give it perfection one should make all the steps on the ball of the feet, without bending the knees on any of them, except, as I have said, it is necessary when beginning the *pas assemblés* to bend a little. This is in order to teach the necessary movements more easily, which are without doubt more agreeable and more noble when they are taken from the hip and foot, but a scholar can do this only after long practice, unless it be with constraint.

ON THE THIRD BRANSLE

THE third is the *Bransle de Poitou* in which the generality only count ten steps, but in order to make it understood with less trouble one should count twelve.

quelque negligence, sans mouuoir la teste, car telles actions ne peuuent qu'anoblir les autres parties de la danse.

DV SECOND BRANSLE

LE second se nomme le Bransle Gay, qui est composé de quatre pas, & se commence à fin de mieux prendre la cadance, par le dernier, en pliant tant soit peu les genoux pour assembler les deux talons en s'esleuant sur la pointe des pieds: Puis pour commencer les quatre pas, faut escarter le pied gauche, & faire que l'autre le suiue de pres contre le talon sur le mouuemẽt du pied, & en releuant la pointe du pied gauche, le lascher doucement à costé en glissant sur le talon, pendant lequel pas glissé, il faut descendre le talon du pied droict plat à terre, & sans s'arreste là dessus, faut plier tant soit peu les genoux pour mieux prẽdre son temps, à fin d'assembler le pied droict au gauche, en se releuãt sur les deux pointes des pieds pour recommencer, & quand on sçaura faire ce Bransle & non plustost, pour en donner la perfection, qu'on face faire tous les pas sur les mouuemens des pieds, sans plier en tout les genoux, que si i'ay dit qu'il faut au commencement faire plier vn peu aux pas assemblez, c'est à fin d'enseigner plus aisément les mouuemens necessaires, qui sont sans doute & plus doux & plus nobles quand ils procedent de la hanche & du pied, mais vn Escolier ne les peut faire qu'apres vn long exercice, du moins qu'auec contrainte.

The METHOD for GENTLEMEN

This *Bransle* begins with a bow which should be made like that of the first, but because the *entrée* of this one is made in sundry ways, I have chosen that which follows as being, in my opinion, the most sedate. Without stopping, then, after the bow, as many do who, lacking a good ear, are obliged to wait in order to choose the proper time to take their cadence, one must start with a step (*temps*) or two in turning before the Lady, according as to how the Music obliges one, in order to finish this *entrée* by a *pas-entre-coupé*.

But so as to proceed well with the rest of the *Bransle*, this *entrée* should finish with the feet separated by half a foot, the toes well outwards, particularly that of the right. Also, in the event of the scholar being already proficient, one must make him glide the whole of this *Bransle* on the ball of the feet, though if he has only begun he must, for the first step, be made to bend his knees a little, and join the right heel to the left in rising on to the toes. Then carry the left foot on the toe to the side, and the right in front. For the fourth, disengage the left foot gently from behind and slide it to the side a half-foot away from the other. On the fifth join them as in the first, and afterwards set off with the left foot in order to glide four steps, the legs very stretched and the movements proceeding from the hip. But because at the ninth step the right foot is in front, it is necessary in making the tenth to slide the left and take it once more to the side, the space of half a foot, and join the right foot to the left. Then to conclude the twelve steps, gently separate the left foot and carry it to the side as in the fourth. And thus continue these same steps face to face with those who dance the *Bransle*, having the hand of the one whom one leads at the side on the waist, until one arrives at whoever occupies the last place; where one must release her, after having turned to the left hand to retake the same course so that, without changing step, he continues as far as the place from where he commenced. At which he should finish by some steps

DV TROISIESME BRANSLE

LE *troisiesme est le Bransle de Poictou, auquel le commun ne compte que dix pas, mais pour le faire comprendre auec moins de peine, il en faut compter douze.*

Ce Bransle se commence par vne reuerence qui se doit faire semblable à celle du premier, mais parce que l'entree de celuy-cy se faict de differentes sortes, i'ay choisi celle qui suit, comme estant à mon opinion la plus graue, sans s'arrester donc apres la reuerence (comme font plusieurs, qui manque de bonne oreille sont contraints d'attendre pour choisir le temps propre à prendre leur cadance.) Il faut partir par vn temps ou deux, en tournant deuant la femme, selon que la Musique obligera, à fin de finir ceste entree par vn pas entrecoupé.

Mais à fin de bien poursuiure le reste du Bransle, ceste entree se doit finir les pieds esloignez de demy pied, les pointes fort ouuertes, principalement celle du droit, & en cas que l'Escolier soit desia auancé, faudra luy faire couler tout ce bransle sur le mouuement des pieds, que s'il ne fait que commencer, il luy faut au premier pas faire plier vn peu les genoüils & assembler le talon droict au gauche, en se releuant sur la pointe des pieds, puis faire porter le pied gauche sur la pointe à costé & le droict deuant. Au quatriesme, desgager doucement le pied gauche de derriere, & le glisser à costé à demy pied de l'autre, & au cinquiesme, assembler comme au premier, & apres faire partir du pied gauche, à fin de faire couler quatre pas, les iambes fort tenduës, & que les mouuemens procedent de la hanche: mais parce qu'au neufiesme pas le pied droict se trouue deuant, il faut pour faire le dixiesme, glisser le gauche & le porter encore vne fois à costé esloigné de

(*temps*) and *pas assemblés*, which he will make in withdrawing from the presence of the lady, which being observed, will leave those in the *Bransle* in good order, and it will be danced without confusion.

The Master should take care that in this *Bransle* the scholar does not always hold the left arm stretched and stiff, as some are in the habit of doing, but make him hold it extended negligently. Make him practise, more especially on the *pas assemblés*, a little movement or bend, which should be made almost, as it were, insensibly, without opening the arms, except a little after the said movement. One should take care also that the scholar never turns the body to the right side and the head to the left, and that he does not mark the cadences with his knees, shoulders, or with the head, and does not drop his eyes—defects which are found frequently in many who are still considered good dancers. But for those who use such actions the Masters, in order to bestow their courtesy, not being willing to offend their judgment, are by no means so blameworthy as those who choose them. And very often these defects come from the scholars who pervert the good movements which are given them, some from having too much affectation, others from too much negligence, and all from not knowing how to judge where such movements should be adopted.

It seems to me useless to speak in detail here of the rest of the *Suite of Bransles*, because, besides that one rarely puts them to use, amusing oneself more in entertainment than in dancing them seriously, the steps and the movements that are to be observed by Ladies, of which I shall speak hereafter, may serve for rules. I will say, nevertheless, that to acquit oneself well, one should make all the movements proceed from the feet and from the hip, unless it be that some Scholar, through weakness, is obliged to bend a little on the *pas assemblés*.

demy pied, & assembler le pied droict au gauche; Puis pour finir les douze pas, escarter doucement le pied gauche, & le porter à costé comme le quatriesme, & ainsi continuer ces mesmes pas face à face de ceux du bransle, ayant la main de laquelle on meine au costé sur la ceincture, iusqu'à ce qu'on paruienne à celuy qui occupe la derniere place, où il la faudra relascher apres auoir tourné sur la main gauche pour reprendre le mesme chemin, à fin que sans changer de pas il continuë iusqu'au lieu où il aura commencé, auquel il doit finir par des temps & des pas assemblez, qu'il fera en se retirant en presence de la femme, ce qu'estant obserué, on laissera ceux du bransle en bel ordre, & sera dansé sans confusion.

Le Maistre doit prẽdre garde qu'en ce brãsle l'Escolier n'y tiẽne pas le bras gauche tousiours roide & tendu, cõme quelques vns souffrẽt faire: mais faisant porter iceluy negligemment estendu. Faire obseruer (principalement aux pas assemblez) vn petit mouuement ou ply, qui se doit faire quasi comme insensiblement sans ouurir les bras, que tres peu apres ledit mouuement. On doit prendre garde aussi que l'Escolier ne tourne point le corps du costé droict & la teste du gauche, & qu'il ny marque les cadances des genoux, des espaules, ny de la teste, & ne porte la veuë basse. Defauts qui se trouuent ordinairement en plusieurs, qui ne laissent d'estre estimez bons danseurs: mais c'est de ceux qui pour gratifier leur courtoisie ne se soucient d'offencer leur iugement, de telles actions les Maistres ne sont nullement blasmables, comme ceux qui les choisissent, & bien souuent ces deffauts viennent des Escoliers qui peruertissent les bonnes actions qu'on leur donne, les vns pour y apporter trop d'affecterie, les autres trop de negligence, & tous ensemble pour ne sçauoir iuger où telles actions se doiuent approprier.

The METHOD for GENTLEMEN

By now all appropriate means have been used to forward the progress of a Gentleman's movements towards a perfect maturity. It seems then, that amongst the good movements the most troublesome are not the least desirable, so that it is proper to proceed with the *Gaillarde*, in which are found certain difficulties. But as the preceding have been conquered by patience, the practice of this also will be rendered easy, providing that one seeks for, and comprehends, the remedies which are proposed, and also that the Master never strays from the Method which is prescribed. I give this last exception to the end that there are some so presumptuous that they think that they possess the highest form of human nature, and therefore wish to regulate everyone to their mould; regarding those ways which are not related to their own as being either sham or false. Nay, indeed, if one praises the grace or ease of movement of another to them, the first thing that they call into consultation is their own judgment, namely their own pattern. But all persons of good sense will find this stupidity insupportable.

ON THE GAILLARDE

TO teach the *Gaillarde* well and with ease, it is first necessary to make a *coupé* with the last step [that is taken] on the right foot, in order to commence with the same [right] foot. After having bent the knees a little, in rising spring on the toe of the left foot, the legs very stretched, and immediately, turning a half-turn only, carry the right foot to the side on the heel, in order to set it at the same instant flat on the ground, and not on the toe of the foot as some do, though the action is ridiculous. Then slide the left on the ball [of the foot] until it comes to the heel of the other to *chassé*. But one must observe that in this *chassé*, the right foot, which is found to be in front, ought to be lifted as soon

❖ METHODE *povr les* CAVALIERS

Il m'a semblé inutile de parler icy par le menu du surplus de la suitte des bransles; Parce qu'outre qu'on ne les met que rarement en vsage, on s'amuse bien plus à s'entretenir qu'à les danser serieusement, d'ailleurs que les pas & les actions qu'on y fait obseruer aux Dames, dont sera parlé cy apres, peuuent seruir de regle. Ie diray toutesfois que pour s'en bien acquitter on doit faire proceder tous les mouuemens des pieds, & de la hanche, si ce n'estoit quelque Escolier auquel pour sa foiblesse on fut obligé faire plier vn peu aux pas assemblez.

Iusques à present qu'on se sera serui de tous les moyens propres pour acheminer les fruicts des actions d'vn Caualier à vne parfaicte maturité: Il semble puis qu'entre les bonnes actions, les plus penibles ne sont pas les moins souhaitables, qu'il est à propos de poursuiure par la Gaillarde, en laquelle se peuuent rencontrer quelques difficultez: mais comme les precedentes auront esté vaincuës par la patience, l'exercice rendra celles-cy facilles, poureuu qu'on recherche & embrasse les remedes qui sont proposez, & que le Maistre ne s'esgare point de la Methode qui luy est prescrite, ie mets ceste derniere exception, pource qu'il y en a de si presomptueux, qu'ils pensent auoir la maistresse forme de l'humaine nature, & ainsi veulent regler tout le monde à leur moule: Estimans que les alleures qui ne se rapportent aux leurs, sont ou feintes, ou fausses; Voire si on leur louë la gentillesse des actions ou facultez de quelque autre: la premiere chose qu'ils appellent à la consultation de leur iugement, c'est leur exemple, mais toutes personnes de bon sens trouueront ceste procedure vne asnerie insuportable.

The METHOD for GENTLEMEN

as the left [joins it]; and at the same time that it is in the air, one must rise off the ground to change feet, raising the left again, which afterwards will make a *coupé* in carrying it forwards gently to disengage the right, which is behind, [to the front.] The whole [sequence] without bending, except to resume in order to begin the same steps again on the other foot, as far as the end of the room, at which one must make a whole turn on the first step in order to retake the same course, so as to return, and finish, from where one had begun, with a bow. I designedly omit to speak in detail of the steps and movements with which it must be finished, forasmuch as the Master will supply these when the scholar will have become capable of dancing in company. Not supposing that there are some who do not know that if the scholar dances high, he should finish by one, or several, *caprioles*; or else by some *temps* in order to take in cadence the action of the bow, which will be spoken of hereafter.

After one is able to perform these *five steps* with ease, and not before, one should learn what kind of arm movements ought to accompany the action of the feet. You must know that in springing the first step it is necessary to open both arms equally to each side, and at the same time that one makes the third step slide behind they must be brought back negligently till the hands, without bending the wrists, come almost together. Then, without stopping on this action, one must lower them in order to carry out the same movements on the fourth and fifth steps; and thus the cadences will be found to be well marked. During all of which actions one must have the toes turned outwards, and the eyes at their own level, so that, holding the body firm and erect, one looks straight at the company, without turning the head, except with the body. And take care never to *chassé* on the toe, nor when making the aforesaid steps, to go from one side of the room to the other, but

METHODE pour les CAVALIERS

DE LA GAILLARDE

POVR *bien & facilement monstrer la Gaillarde, il faut premierement faire couper le dernier pas du pied droict, à fin de commencer du mesme pied, apres auoir vn peu plié les genoüils, faut en se leuant sauter sur la pointe du pied gauche, les iambes fort tenduës, & incontinent porter (en tournant demy tour seulement) le pied droict à costé sur le talon, à fin de l'assoir tout à l'instant plat à terre, & non sur la pointe du pied, comme quelques vns font pratiquer, quoy que l'action en soit ridicule, puis faire couler le gauche sur le mouuement d'iceluy, iusqu'à ce qu'il paruienne au talon de l'autre pour chasser, mais faut obseruer qu'en ce chassé le pied droict qui se trouue deuant doit leuer aussi tost que le gauche, & en mesme temps qu'il sera en l'air, il faut en s'esleuant hors terre changer de pied, releuant le gauche, duquel par apres sera coupé en le portant deuant, pour desgager doucement le droict qui se trouue derriere, le tout sans plier que pour se reprendre, à fin de recommencer de l'autre pied les mesmes pas iusqu'au bout de la salle, où estant, il faudra faire sur le premier pas vn tour entier pour reprendre le mesme chemin, à fin de reuenir finir par vne reuerence où on aura commencé: i'obmets à dessein à dire par le menu les pas & les actions auec lesquelles il faut finir, d'autant que le Maistre les suppleera lors que l'Escolier sera capable de danser en compagnie, n'estimant pas qu'il y en aye qui ignorent, que si l'Escolier va par haut il doit finir par vne ou plusieurs caprioles, sinon par quelque temps, pour prendre en cadance l'action de la reuerence, dont sera parlé cy apres.*

Apres qu'on pourra faire facilement ces cinq pas, il faudra apprendre (& non plustost,) de quelle sorte le

The METHOD for GENTLEMEN

keep a straight line as much as possible; this will be very easy if one makes the steps to the side and not in front.

Now forasmuch as there are some people who, having too short a foot or bandy legs, howbeit that the rest of the body be well fashioned or proportioned, can never gain a true reputation for good dancing, there are likewise others who sympathise so much with the ground that they can scarcely abandon it. It is very necessary, therefore, that they shall rank with those who, for their honour, are obliged to dance *terre-à-terre*; for although they lack not the disposition, nevertheless they have too bad a grace to dance high. For, in fact, a man should never mix *caprioles*, particularly for the sake of a reputation, if he does not excel therein: or if he does not wish to provide sport for the company, as some do who, being unable to display the deportment and decency of our nobility, seek to commend themselves by leaps and other exaggerated movements. So much so that I counsel such persons, when performing the *Gaillarde*, to abide by the above-named *five-steps*, which, when done with a becoming grace, are better than a heap of passages that one knows how to make, but which put one too much in mind of a juggler.

ON THE CAPRIOLE

ALTHOUGH it appears that to *Capriole*, or to dance high, is an action very violent, hard, and troublesome to acquire, by practising it as is required, and observing that which I shall say hereafter, one can render it as easy as the minor actions which are practised in dancing.

But because those who have attained perfection in it have in all probability begun long since, it is greatly necessary that those who undertake it should not wait till a too advanced age. Otherwise that which is possible to acquire

mouuement des bras doit accompagner l'action des pieds, c'est qu'en sautãt le premier pas il faut ouurir les bras esgalemẽt chacun de son costé, & en mesme temps qu'on fera glisser le troisiesme pas derriere, faut les rapporter negligemment, iusqu'à ce que les mains sans plier le poignet viennent quasi à se ioindre, lors sans s'arrester sur ceste action il faudra descendre, à fin d'obseruer au quatriesme & cinquiesme les mesmes mouuemens, & ainsi les cadances se trouueront bien marquees: Pendant toutes lesquelles actions il faut auoir les pointes des pieds ouuertes & la veuë de sa hauteur, à fin que tenant le corps droict & ferme on regarde en face la compagnie, sans tourner la teste qu'auec le corps, & prendre garde à ne point chasser de la pointe du pied, ny en faisant les pas susdits, aller de l'vne à l'autre extremité du lieu: mais y tenir la droicte ligne le plus qu'il sera possible, ce qui sera fort aisé, si on faict porter les pas de costé, non deuant soy.

Or comme il y a des personnes qui pour auoir le pied trop court, ou les iambes faictes en paranteze, quoy que le reste du corps soit bien taillé ou proportionné, ne peuuent iamais venir à vne vraye reputation de bien danser. Ainsi en y a-il d'autres qui sympatisent si fort auec la terre, qu'ils ne la peuuent iamais abandonner que de bien peu: C'est pourquoy il est fort à propos qu'ils se rangent auec ceux lesquels, bien qu'ils ne manquent point de disposition, neanmoins pour auoir trop mauuaise grace à la dãse par haut, sont pour leur honneur contraints d'aller terre à terre: Car en effect vn homme ne se doit iamais mesler de caprioler, principalement en lieu de reputation, s'il n'excelle, ou s'il ne veut seruir de ioüet à la compagnie, comme font aucuns, qui ne pouuant representer le port & la descence de nostre noblesse, cher-

The METHOD for GENTLEMEN

almost insensibly by length of time, by being hastened could only be overcome with great difficulty; and perhaps they would find themselves in the end at the foot of a wall with no ladder. It being very true that those who dance best have brought to it no other skill than long and assiduous practice, which alone brings into play those springs which produce the softness of so many divers movements by which the dance is seen to be ennobled.

It is necessary therefore, in order to combine grace with the action, to observe in commencing it that one ought never to bend the knees, except when one wishes to take the *temps* for rising. Forasmuch as it is necessary that all these movements should come from the hip, and that on all of them the toes [pointing downwards and] well lifted [off the ground,] should, in crossing, reach to the heel [of the other foot]. And in this fashion to cross by degrees, first to two, then to three, and thus continue; always holding the body firm and erect, without shaking the head, having the toes a little outwards, as much in rising as in descending, and fall with one [foot] near enough to the other in order to repeat it more easily. To be less arduous, one can use a table, or two chairs to sustain oneself by the strength of the arms. Then, in coming to practise without support, in raising oneself for the first one must carry the hands as far as the busk of the pourpoint, like those who take their strength to make a leap, and on the second, bring them down, opening the arms a little; and thus continue, always keeping the eyes level with your height, without stooping. And when one will reach the point of being able to cross six, it is necessary to stop and practise this well in order to do it easily. For it is very true that in crossing to seven, or eight, does not appear any advantage. On the contrary, one only grazes the legs from the knees down, besides that it is impossible to do more than a few in succession, because the actions are then usually strained. So much so that it

chent à se recommander par des fauts & autres mouuemens battelleresques: tellement que ie conseille telles personnes à se tenir pour le faict de la Gaillarde aux cinq pas susdits, lesquels faicts de bonne grace, valent mieux qu'vn tas de passages qu'on sçauroit faire, qui sentent par trop son baladin.

DE LA CAPRIOLE

*E*T *bien qu'il semble que Caprioler ou aller par haut soit vne action fort violente, penible, & tres malaisee à acquerir, si est-ce que s'y exerçant, comme il est requis, & y obseruant ce que i'en diray cy apres, on se la pourra rendre aussi facile que les moindres actions qui se pratiquent en la danse.*

Mais parce que ceux qui en ont atteint la perfection y ont auec plus d'apparence commencé de longue main, il est grandement necessaire que ceux qui l'entreprendront n'attendent point à vn aage trop auancé, autrement ce qui se pourroit quasi acquerir insensiblement par succession de temps, venant à estre precipité ne se pourroit vaincre qu'auec grande difficulté, & peut estre se trouueroient ils au bout de leur compte, au pied d'vn mur sans eschelle, estant tres-veritable que les mieux dansans n'y ont pas apporté d'autre finesse qu'vn long & assidu exercice, qui seul fait ioüer en eux ces ressorts qui produisent la douceur de tant de diuers mouuemens dont la danse se voit annoblie.

Il faut donc obseruer en y commençant (à fin de ioindre la grace à l'action) que l'on ne doit iamais plier les genoüils que lors qu'on veut prendre son temps pour s'esleuer, d'autant qu'il faut que tous les mouuemens procedent de la hanche, & qu'à chacun d'iceux la pointe des pieds (fort releuee) paruienne en la passant

The METHOD for GENTLEMEN

would be better to cross only up to four on both feet, and that this be done with ease.

For the rest, when the scholar shall be capable of dancing in company, one must make him learn the following actions for asking a lady to dance. Having therefore removed his hat, which he will hold on the busk of the pourpoint, he will take some sedate steps; after which, approaching her, he will slide the right foot gently before the other in order to make a bow like that whereof I have spoken for accosting a company. Then, lowering his head a little with his body in order to kiss his hand and to take that of the Lady, he will lead her to the lower end, facing the company. Whereupon he will make a bow, such as one has instructed him for the *Courante*, then, retaking the Lady by the hand, he will conduct her as far as the middle of the room. And if there be there any person of quality, he will repeat the same bow; if not, he only salutes the lady. Then making his way towards the right hand, replacing his hat, he will make three or four steps, in the manner that has been said above, before taking the cadence in order to begin. Then, having finished, that a bow be made before the Lady, but first it must not be forgotten to make one before the company, in case, as I have told you, there be any to whom you are obliged. Neither forget to lead the Lady to her place, all with steps and gait which are not timid.

au talon, & de ceste façon la passer par degrez premierement à deux, puis à trois, & ainsi continuer, tenant tousiours le corps ferme & droict sans bransler la teste, ayant la pointe des pieds, tant en s'esleuant qu'en descendant vn peu ouuerte, & tomber l'vn assez pres de l'autre, à fin de se mieux reprendre, & pour moins de peine, on se peut seruir d'vne table, ou de deux chaises pour se soustenir sur la force des bras, puis venant à s'exercer sans appuy en s'esleuant à la premiere, faut porter les mains iusques au busque du pourpoint, comme qui prendroit sa force pour faire vn saut, & à la seconde, les descendre ouurant vn peu les bras, & ainsi continuer, tenant tousiours la veuë esgale de sa hauteur sans se courber, & quand on sera paruenu à ce poinct de la pouuoir passer à six, il s'y faut arrester, & s'y exercer fort, à fin de la faire facilement, car il est tres vray que passee à sept, ou à huict, elle n'en paroit pas d'auantage, au contraire on ne fait que frisotter du genoüil en bas, outre qu'il est impossible d'en faire que fort peu de suitte, dont les actions sont ordinairement forcees, si bien qu'il vaudroit mieux ne la passer qu'à quatre sur les deux pieds, & que ce fut auec facilité.

Au surplus, lors que l'Escolier sera capable de danser en compagnie, il luy faut apprendre les actions qui suiuent pour prier vne Dame de danser; Ayant donc tiré le chapeau, qu'il portera sur le busque du pourpoint, il fera quelques demarches graues, apres lesquelles venant à s'approcher, il coulera doucement le pied droict deuant l'autre, pour faire vne reuerence, comme celle dont i'ay parlé pour aborder vne compagnie, & baissant vn peu la teste auec le corps, pour baiser la main & prendre celle de la femme, il l'amenera au bas bout, vis à vis de la compagnie, où estant il fera vne reuerence, comme on luy a enseigné

The METHOD for GENTLEMEN

ON THE BOW IN ORDER TO SALUTE A LORD OR A LADY

IF one wishes to give a scholar the gravity which is required to salute a Lord or a Lady, one must make him practise the following bows frequently.

It is first necessary, as I have already said for the first bow, to remove the hat. After making some sedate steps, without affectation, and when that one comes near to him one wishes to salute, the right leg, well stretched, must slide before the left, and at the same time, in bending the knees, not forwards but outwards to each side, bend the waist also. Thus, without lowering the head except with the body, the right arm being well extended, lower all equally, as much or as little as the quality of whomsoever one wishes to salute obliges. And without stopping on this action, in rising, one must kiss the right hand, then, carrying it back to its place, separate the left foot at once to the side and slide the right behind, where it will be disengaged gently in bending just a little, and thereupon stop to converse.

These same actions should be observed by a Gentleman in order to salute a Lady, except that he should, in rising, after having kissed his hand, also kiss the Lady. Then disengage the left foot and slide the right behind, which he must bring back by sliding it gently, as has been said above in saluting a Gentleman.

There are besides certain actions which one includes among the ceremonies, or compliments, which a visit, approaching or receiving company obliges one to make, which, provided that one forgets them with discreetness and not by error, on account of being sometimes too tedious or importunate, one shall not thereby lose grace.

Now since the aforesaid dances are without doubt the most accepted, so also they bring with more benefit some

à la Courante, puis reprenant la femme par la main, la conduira iusques au milieu de la salle, & là s'il y a quelque personne qualifiee il refera la mesme reuerence, sinon qu'il saluë la femme seulement: Puis prenant son chemin vers la main droicte en remettant son chapeau, fera trois, ou quatre demarches, de la façon qu'il a esté dict cy dessus, auant que prendre la cadance pour commencer, & venant à finir, que ce soit d'vne reuerence deuant la Dame, mais ne faut pas oublier d'en faire vne auparauant deuant la compagnie, en cas qu'il y ait comme ie vous ay dict, quelqu'vn qui vous y obligeast, ny à ramener la Dame en sa place, le tout auec des pas & des demarches qui ne soient pas timides.

DE LA REVERENCE POVR SALVER VN SEIGNEVR OV VNE DAME

QVE *si on veut donner à vn Escolier la grauité qui est requise pour salüer vn Seigneur, ou vne Dame, qu'on luy face souuent prattiquer les reuerences qui suiuent.*

Il faut premierement, comme i'ay desia dict à la premiere reuerence, tirer le chapeau, & apres faire quelques demarches graues sans affecterie, & lors qu'on viendra à ioindre celuy qu'on veut salüer, faut la iambe bien tenduë glisser le pied droict deuant le gauche, & en mesme temps, pliant les genoüils non en auant, mais en dehors chacun de son costé, plier aussi de la ceinture, & ainsi (sans baisser la teste qu'auec le corps) le bras droict bien estendu, descendre le tout esgalement, tant & si peu que la qualité de celuy qu'on saluë pourra obliger, & sans s'arrester sur ceste action, en se releuant faut baiser la main droicte,

honour of the profit which one can acquire by learning them. Whosoever follows that which I have taught, will be assured of having acquired an action which is wholly becoming. Also sufficient knowledge not to allow himself to be spoiled by bad habits in the event of his curiosity leading him to practise those dances which are in less request, which will not be spoken of at present, for as much as the principal object which I have aimed at has only been to give the scholar grace and modesty, for which the rest of the dances are useless.

METHODE *povr les* CAVALIERS

& la raportant à son naturel, escarter aussi tost le pied gauche à costé, & glisser le droict derriere, qu'il faudra desgager doucement en pliant tant soit peu, & là dessus s'arrester pour s'entretenir.

Ces mesmes actions doiuent estre oberuees par vn Caualier pour salüer vne Dame, excepté qu'il faut en se releuant apres auoir baisé la main, baiser aussi la Dame, puis desgager le pied gauche & glisser le droict derriere, qu'il faudra rapporter, en le glissant doucement, comme il a esté dict cy dessus, pour salüer vn Caualier.

Il y a au reste certaines actions qu'on mesle parmy les ceremonies ou complimens, qu'vne, visite, abort, ou reception d'vne compagnie oblige faire, qui pour estre quelquefois trop ennuyeuses, ou importunes, pourueu qu'on les oublie par discretion, non par erreur, on n'en à pas moins de grace.

Or comme les susdites danses sont sans doute les plus receuës: aussi apportent elles auec plus d'auantage quelque honneur du profit qu'on peut faire en leur escole, & quiconque suiura ce que i'en ay enseigné qu'il s'asseure d'en acquerir vne action toute belle, & assez de cognoissance pour ne la laisser corrompre par mauuaises habitudes, en cas que sa curiosité le portast à l'exercice des danses moins requises, desquelles il ne sera pas parlé quand à present, d'autant que le but principal où i'ay visé, n'a esté que de donner à vn Escolier la grace & la modestie, à quoy le surplus des danses sont inutiles.

A MADAME LA MARQVISE DE BVCKINGHAM, &c.

MADAME,
Si vous considerez que toutes choses tendent necessairement à leur centre, ie m'asseure que vous ne trouuerez pas estrange que ce discours s'ose adresser à vostre grandeur, puis qu'il la recognoist pour l'élement & le vray seiour des graces dont il traicte, on ne peut en cela l'accuser d'effronterie ny d'imprudence, (car il ne pouuoit resister à la Nature, qui l'oblige de rechercher en vostre faueur la conseruation de la vie que ie luy donne, ny s'asseurer contre les attaques de l'ennuie, qu'en vostre protection. Toute sa felicité (MADAME) *depend du bon accueil que vostre grandeur luy fera, & la mienne du temps auquel ie pourray contribuer à la recognoissance de vos perfections quelque preuue plus digne de la qualité,*

MADAME,
De vostre tres-humble & tres-obeissant seruiteur,

F. De Lavze.

TO MY LADY MARCHIONESS OF BUCKINGHAM

MY LADY,
If you consider that all things tend necessarily towards their centre, I am assured that you will not find it strange that this discourse dares to be addressed to your Ladyship, since it acknowledges in you the principal and true abode of the graces of which it treats. It cannot in this be accused either of effrontery or of imprudence, for it could not resist Nature which obliges it to seek in your favour the preservation of the life I give it. Nor could it be assured, except by your protection, against malicious attacks. All its felicity, my Lady, depends on the good reception which your Ladyship will give it, and all mine on the time when I will be able to contribute to the recognition of your perfections, some proof more worthy of their quality,

Your Ladyship's very humble and very obedient servant,
F. DE LAUZE.

METHODE POVR LES DAMES

IL est indubitable que la beauté des Dames a seruy de subiect aux enuieux, pour blasmer cest exercice: Car disent ils, si les perfections d'vn beau visage armé desia de mil mignardises & d'appas sont anoblies des graces de la danse, y aura il des yeux assez chastes pour soustenir l'esclat de tant de traits & d'atraits sans alarmes. Mais voyez mes Dames la responce que ie leur ay faicte en l'Apologie de ce traité, où vous aprendrez que l'on s'offence à tort d'vne intention innocente, & qu'il n'y a que les circonstances des temps & des lieux qui puissent rendre vos actions blasmables, ce que si vous considerez bien, vous n'attacherez iamais vostre creance à ces superstitieuses persuasions. Quitez donc ces opinions anticipees, & suiuez ces pas, qui seuls vous peuuent acheminer à la bien-seance, vous asseurant que si vous les accompagnez de la grauité, & de la modestie (deux graces principales qui doiuent tousiours regler vos actions) vous receurez du fruict de mes enseignemens vn contentement incroyable.

Plusieurs maistres estiment qu'il n'est pas necessaire d'obliger vne Dame à porter les pointes des pieds ouuertes, & se fondent seulement sur ce que n'estant pas subiectes à estre veuës, il n'importe qu'elle action elles ayent.

Ie suiurois certes en cela leur opinion pour le soulagement de celles qu'vne mauuaise habitude contraint à les porter en dedans, si l'experience ne me donnoit loy de soustenir le contraire.

Car comme on ne me sçauroit nyer que l'action du

THE METHOD FOR LADIES

IT is indubitable that the beauty of Ladies has served as a subject to the envious to censure this exercise. For, they say, if the perfections of a beautiful face, already armed with a thousand delicacies and allurements, are ennobled with the graces of the dance, will there be eyes chaste enough to withstand the radiance of so many attractions and enticements without alarm. But look you, my Ladies, at the reply which I have given them in the *Apologie* of this treatise, where you will learn that one becomes wrongly offended through an innocent intention; and that it is only the circumstances of time and place which could render your actions blameworthy. Thus, if you reflect well, you will never attach your belief to these superstitious persuasions. Forsake then these prejudices, and follow these steps, which alone will lead you to walk with decorum. Assuring you that if you accompany them with gravity and modesty, two principal graces which should always regulate your actions, you will receive from the results of my instructions an incredible satisfaction.

Many masters consider that it is not necessary to oblige a Lady to turn her toes outwards, and this is founded merely in that, as they are not subjected to view, it matters not what action they have.

I would follow, indeed, in their opinion for the ease of those who, from bad habit, are compelled to turn them inwards, if experience had not given me the authority to uphold the contrary.

Forasmuch as no one will deny me that the action of the body in dancing naturally follows that of the feet, I am assured that if they pay attention to the movements which

corps ne suiue naturellement en dansant celle des pieds, ie m'asseure si on prend garde aux mouuemens qui se font tant des espaules que du reste du corps, en les ouurant & fermant, ou si on fait comparaison de la grace de quelqu'vne qui en dansant à les pointes des pieds en dedans, auec celle qu'elle aura les ayant ouuertes qu'on aprouuera mon aduis.

DES PRINCIPES

E*T pource que le visage d'vne Dame est le premier obiect qui attire les yeux des regardans pour iuger de sa grace, il faut en premier lieu s'estudier à luy bien placer la teste & regler sa veuë, qui doit tousiours estre esgalle de sa hauteur en dansant, puis luy faire mettre les pieds assez pres l'vn de l'autre, les pointes ouuertes, & ainsi la tenant par les deux mains, luy faire faire quelques demarches graues & en droicte ligne, pour luy aquerir l'air auec lequel elle doit aborder ou receuoir vne compagnie, cela gaigné qu'elle aprene à faire la reuerence en ceste sorte.*

DE LA REVERENCE

L*ORS que sa discretion luy fera iuger le temps de saluer la compagnie qu'elle reçoit ou qu'elle aborde, il faut qu'elle escarte tant soit peu l'vn des pieds à costé, & d'vn mesme temps glisser doucement l'autre quasi tout ioignant, les pointes ouuertes, lors sans s'arrester que bien peu, ayant les bras negligement estendus sur les costez, elle doit auec le plus de douceur qu'il sera possible plier esgalement les deux*

The METHOD *for* LADIES

are made, as much with the shoulders as with the rest of the body, when opening and closing [the feet], or if they make a comparison between the grace of one who, in dancing, keeps the toes turned in with she who will have them outwards, that they will approve of my advice.

ON PRINCIPLES

AND for the reason that the face of a Lady is the first object which draws the eyes of the beholders, in order to judge her grace one must in the first place endeavour to set her head, and to regulate her eyes, which should always be level with one's height when dancing. Then make her put her feet close to one another, the toes outwards, and thus holding her by the hands make her take some steps, sedately and in a straight line, in order that she may acquire the manner in which she should approach, or receive, company. That being accomplished, she may then learn how to make a curtsy in this manner.

ON THE CURTSY

WHEN her discretion shall enable her to judge the occasion to salute the company which she is receiving or approaching, she must move one foot a little to the side, and at the same time gently slide the other almost joining [the first], with the toes outwards. Then, only pausing a little, and having the arms negligently extended to the sides, she should, with the utmost smoothness that is possible, bend both knees equally, not in front as many do, who by holding their toes together acquit themselves very badly, but out to each side. If she wishes to descend very

genoüils, non en auãt comme font plusieurs, qui pour tenir les pointes des pieds closes s'en aquittent assez mal, mais chacun de son costé, & si elle la desire descendre tres-basse & y tenir quand & quand le corps droit & ferme, qu'elle leue doucement les talons en se soutenant sur la pointe des pieds à mesure qu'elle pliera les genoüils, & lors qu'elle l'aura tiree au point qu'elle la voudra faire, faut tout aussi tost luy faire remonter de mesme air qu'elle aura descendu. Mais il faut luy aprendre que selon les occasions elle les doit faire plus ou moins humbles, y obseruant toutesfois vne mediocrité, à fin qu'on ne la puisse blasmer d'affecterie, au reste il est necessaire en la commençant de regarder en face la compagnie, mais pour ne s'esloigner de la modestie, en pliãt les genoüils faut faire descendre la veuë auec le corps qu'on releuera en finissant, sans l'arrester à regarder personne fixement en face, pource que cela tient de l'effronterie.

Et parce qu'en faisant des visites il se rencontre quelque fois diuerses compagnies en vn mesme lieu, lesquelles vne Dame est obligee (soit par bienseance ou autrement) de salüer simplement en passant, & aussi qu'il seroit ennuieux de faire tousiours vne profonde reuerance, principalement parmy les complimens ceremonieux qui se font en telles occasions, ou aux ceremonies d'vn depart apres le premier congé pris d'vne compagnie, ie diray comme il s'en faut acquitter.

Premierement apres qu'on aura fait vne reuerence de pied ferme auant qu'aborder vne compagnie, comme il a esté dict cy dessus, il faut selon que les personnes seront placees porter (chemin faisant) vn pas de costé en se tournant vis à vis de ceux qu'on salüe, que si la compagnie est à main droicte, que ce soit du pied gauche, & si à gauche, du droict, & en mesme temps

The METHOD *for* LADIES

low and remain there a while, the body firm and erect, then she will raise her heels, supporting herself on her toes while she bends her knees. And when she has sunk to the degree that she would make, she must be made to rise again, according to the manner in which she went down. But one must teach her that she should make these [curtsies] more or less humble, according to the occasion; observing, nevertheless, a middle course, to the end that none can reproach her with affectation. Furthermore, when she begins it, it is necessary to look at the company, but in order not to depart from modesty, in bending the knees she must lower the eyes with the body, which, on finishing, will be raised again, without stopping to regard any person fixedly, for that savours of effrontery.

And because when making visits, one sometimes encounters various assemblies in the same place, to whom, whether from decorum or otherwise, a Lady is merely obliged to make a curtsy in passing; and also that it would be irksome to make a profound curtsy continually, principally among the ceremonial compliments which are made on such occasions: and again at the ceremonies of leave-taking, after the first curtsy is made to the company: I will state how she should acquit herself therein.

Firstly, after she has made a curtsy with the feet together before approaching a company, as has been said above, she must take, while walking, a step to the side, according to how the persons are placed, turning to face those whom she salutes. So that if the company be to the right hand, this be made with the left foot, and if on the left, with the right, and at the same time slide the other quite leisurely in front. Without stopping on this action, after having smoothly and only slightly bent the knees, she should rise again as she dropped, in sliding, as it were insensibly, the foot which is behind, on which she will make the first step in order to continue her way. She ought,

glisser tout à loisir l'autre deuant, & sans s'arrester sur ceste action, apres auoir doucement & bien peu plié les deux genoüils, il faut faire releuer de mesme qu'on aura descendu, en glissant comme insensiblement le pied qui se trouuera derriere, duquel on fera le premier pas pour continuer son chemin; On doit au surplus faire exercer souuent ceste mesme reuerence sur l'vn & sur l'autre pied, & faire cognoistre qu'il est tres à propos de la faire de ceste sorte en presence de ceux auec lesquels on s'entretient, à fin qu'aux occasions on ne soit pas surpris, & qu'auec vne grace asseuree on puisse s'en acquitter dignement.

Et d'autant que les danses les plus vsitees sont les plus nobles & necessaires, & par consequent plus sortables à mon dessein, & que pour s'acquitter dignement d'icelles, les pas & les démarches plus naturelles sont non seulement les plus requises aux Dames, mais sans comparaison les plus propres pour leur acquerir vn port naïf, & vne action bien plus belle, qu'vn meslange confus de diuerses decoupeures & agitation de corps esloigné de toute bien seance, & que les bransles qui sont tous plains de grauité & de modestie, sont aussi plus propres pour leur asseurer la grace & adoucir l'air: ce n'est pas sans raison que ie veux commencer par là.

DV PREMIER BRANSLE

IE diray donc que le Bransle simple composé de huict pas, (apres auoir faict la reuerence telle que ie la viens de d'escrire, qui sera commencee du pied droict, tant deuant la compagnie qu'en tournant deuant vn Caualier,) se commence du pied gauche qu'on portera à costé, à la pointe duquel (la iambe

The METHOD *for* LADIES

moreover, to practise this same curtsy frequently, on one foot and then the other, and let it be known that it is very appropriate to perform it in this way in the presence of those with whom one converses, so that she shall not be surprised on such occasions, but that with an assured grace, she may acquit herself with dignity.

And forasmuch as the most fashionable dances are the most noble and necessary, and in consequence more suitable to my purpose; and that in order to acquit oneself with dignity in them, the most natural steps and paces are not only the most requisite for Ladies, but are without comparison more fitted to make them acquire a natural carriage and a graceful action than a confused medley of divers *découpures* and agitations of the body, altogether removed from all decorum. So, as the *Bransles* which are full of gravity and modesty are also most proper to ensure a soft and graceful air, it is not without reason that I wish to commence with these.

ON THE FIRST BRANSLE

I SAY then, that the *Bransle Simple* is composed of eight steps. After having made the curtsy, such as that which I have just described, which will be begun on the right foot, as well before the company as in turning towards the Gentleman, begin with the left foot, which one will carry to the side; to the toe of which, the right foot will be made to slide, without effort, the leg being very stretched. At the same time make the left shoulder turn outwards a very little, without swaying the body, for the action of the foot is alone sufficient if the toe is well turned outward. Then, in order to make the third step, disengage the left foot and carry it level with the other, separated by the length of a half-foot only, and on this raise the body all-in-one-piece

bien tenduë) on fera glisser sans effort le pied droict sur le mouuement d'iceluy, en faisant d'vn mesme temps tourner tant soit peu l'espaule gauche en dehors, sans esbranler le corps, car la seule action du pied suffit, si la pointe en est bien ouuerte ; Puis pour faire le troisiesme pas faut desgager le pied gauche, & le porter esgal à l'autre, esloigné de demy pied seulement, & là dessus en esleuant le corps tout d'vne piece sur le mouuement des pieds, assembler en glissant le talon droict au gauche, & au cinquiesme porter le gauche à costé, esloigné comme le premier, puis pour faire le sixiesme glisser seulement le droict iusqu'à ce qu'il paruienne derriere au talon de l'autre, alors sans plier en tout les genoüils, s'esleuant tãt soit peu sur la pointe du pied qui se trouue derriere, faut porter le septiesme pas à costé, esgal & esloigné comme le troisiesme, & finir par vn pas qu'on glissera du pied droict à la pointe de l'autre, semblable au deuxiesme, à fin de recommencer.

Mais à fin qu'il n'y ait rien à dire aux actions de celles qui danseront ce Bransle, il faut que le corps & la teste y soient tenus droicts & fermes, en sorte que tous les mouuemens procedent de la hanche & des pieds, sans hausser en tout les espaules ny plier les genoüils, du moins que tres peu, à fin que les actions n'en soient forcees, les pointes des pieds ouuertes, & que les trois premiers pas soient assis plats à terre, & tout le reste sur le mouuement des pieds, excepté le dernier, comme i'ay desia dict, tenant tousiours la veuë esgale de sa hauteur, l'action de laquelle ne doit tourner qu'auec le corps, sans aucun mouuement de la teste.

The METHOD for LADIES

on to the ball of both feet, joining them by sliding the right heel to the left. For the fifth carry the left to the side, separated as in the first. Then to make the sixth, slide the right only so far that it reaches behind the heel of the other. After that, without bending the knees at all, in rising a very little on to the toe of the foot which is behind, one must carry the seventh step to the side, level with the previous one and separated as in the third. And finish by a step which one will slide with the right foot to the toe of the other, like unto the second, in order to begin again.

But, to the end that there will be nothing left to say about the actions of those who will dance this *Bransle*, the body and head should be held erect and firm, so that all the movements proceed from the hip and the feet, without jogging the shoulders, neither bending the knees, except just a little so that the actions will not be stiff; and the toes outwards. Also that the first three steps be placed flat on the ground, and all the rest on the ball of the feet, except the last, as I have already said. Always keep the eyes level with one's own height, the action of which should not be turned except with the body, without any movement of the head.

ON THE BRANSLE GAY

AS has been said for a Gentleman, it is necessary that the Lady also begins the *Bransle Gay* by the last step, in order to get the cadence. To do this, bend the knees a little, and draw the right heel, by sliding it, to join the left, rising on to the toes of both feet. Then, to begin the first of the four steps of which it is composed, one must separate the left foot to the side, and at the same time make the other follow it closely, until it comes to the heel. For the third, without bending the knees, gently slide the left foot to the

METHODE *povr les* DAMES

DV BRANSLE GAY

TOVT *de mesmes qu'il a esté dict pour vn Caualier, il faut qu'vne Dame commence le Bransle Gay par le dernier pas, à fin de bien prendre la cadance, & pour ce faire en pliant tant soit peu les genoüils, on assemblera le talon droict au gauche en glissant, & se releuant sur la pointe de tous les deux ; Puis commençant le premier des quatre pas dõt il est composé, il faut escarter le pied gauche à costé, & faire que d'vn mesme temps l'autre le suiue de pres en glissant, iusqu'à ce qu'il paruienne au talon, & au troisiesme sans plier les genoüils, glisser doucement le pied gauche à costé sur le talon la pointe releuee, puis en pliãt les genoüils, assembler comme on aura faict pour prendre la cadance, à fin de recommencer.*

Il faut toutes fois notter qu'à tous les pas assemblez de ce bransle, & non ailleurs (pour ne rien forcer, & danser sans contrainte,) il faut plier tant soit peu les genoüils, mais il est sur tout necessaire de se releuer sur la pointe des pieds, & si quelquefois pour diuersifier on veut faire glisser au deuxiesme pas le pied droict derriere, en sorte que le corps tournant vn peu du costé de celuy qu'on meine, la veuë tourne aussi & non autremẽt, on le pourra faire, sans leur permettre, comme font plusieurs de regarder par dessus les espaules, ny certains branslemens de corps, que quelques vns y font obseruer, dont les actions sont fort desagreables.

DV BRANSLE DE POICTOV

LE *troisiesme est le bransle de Poictou, où il faut compter douze pas, lequel se commence (apres vne reuerence qu'on fera semblable à celle du premier,) par*

The METHOD for LADIES

side on the heel, the toe raised. Then, bending the knees, join [the feet] as one did in order to take the cadence, so that it may be repeated.

They must always note that for all the *pas assemblés* in this *Bransle*, and not otherwise, so as to dance without constraint and stiffness, one must bend the knees a little, but it is necessary above all to rise on to the toes. And if sometimes for a diversion they wish to slide the right foot behind on the second step, in a manner so that the body turns a little to the side of him whom one leads, they may do this, turning the eyes also, but not otherwise, without permitting them to look over their shoulders as some do. Neither let there be certain shakings of the body, such as some are seen to do, whose actions are very disagreeable.

ON THE BRANSLE DE POITOU

THE third is the *Bransle de Poitou*, where one must count twelve steps. Which, after the curtsy which will be made as for the first [*Bransle*], begins by a *temps* or two, with one or more sliding steps in turning before him whom one leads, according to how the music obliges one to take the cadence.

This *entrée* should finish with the feet separated about half a foot, and then, holding the right hand on the waist at the side, one must continue face to face with all those in the *Bransle*, by the following steps.

Firstly, bend the knees a little, and gather, with a slide, the right heel to the left, rising on to the toes, and without stopping thereupon, carry the left foot to the side and the right in front on the ball of both feet. Then, for the fourth, disengaging the left foot, slide it gently a half-foot distant from the other, and on the fifth join the feet as for the first, the legs very stretched. And because on the ninth the right

METHODE *pour les* DAMES

vn temps ou deux, auec vn ou plusieurs pas coulez, en tournant deuant celuy qu'on meine, selon que la Musique pourra obliger pour prendre la cadence.

Ceste entree se doit finir les pieds esloignez d'enuiron demy pied, & lors portant la main droicte au costé sur la ceinture, il faut poursuiure face à face de tous ceux du bransle sur les pas qui suiuent.

Premierement, il faut plier vn peu les genoüils & assembler (en glissant) le talon droict au gauche, en se releuant sur la pointe des pieds, & sans s'arrester là dessus, porter le pied gauche à costé, & le droict deuant sur le mouuement d'iceux, puis au quatriesme, en desgageant le pied gauche, le glisser doucement à demy pied de l'autre, & au cinquiesme, assembler comme au premier, pour puis apres couler quatre pas sur le mouuement des pieds, les iambes bien tendües, & parce qu'au neufiesme le pied droict se trouue deuant, il faut glisser le pied gauche à costé pour assembler encore vne fois le droict, à fin de desgager au douziesme le pied gauche, comme au quatriesme pour recommencer, & ainsi continuer sur ces mesmes pas.

Et lors qu'on sera paruenu à celuy qui occupe la derniere place du bransle, faut tourner sur la main gauche, & reprendre à peu pres le chemin qu'on aura faict en relaschant la main du costé, & ouurir les bras, pour mener auec plus de liberté, & ainsi on pourra finir par vne reuerence, & laisser la compagnie en bel ordre, ce qui se doit faire en cadance, mais auparauant la reuerence, on peut finir en ceste sorte.

Apres auoir assemble le premier pas du pied droict en glissant, & escarté vn peu le gauche à costé tournant deuant celuy qu'on meine, faire deux pas lentement en arriere, s'esleuant sur le mouuement du pied qui sera à terre, puis en pliant vn peu les genoüils,

The METHOD for LADIES

foot is found to be in front, one must slide the left to the side, so that the right may be joined to it once again. Finally, for the twelfth, disengage the left foot as for the fourth, in order to begin again; and thus continue with these same steps.

Then, when she has reached whoever occupies the last place in the *Bransle*, she must turn to the left hand, and retrace almost the same course that she has made, at the same time releasing the hand from the side, and opening the arms, in order to lead with greater freedom. Thus she may finish with a curtsy, and to leave the company in good order, this should be made in cadence. But previous to making the curtsy, she may finish in this manner.

After having joined the first step with the right foot in sliding, and having separated the left a little to the side in turning before him whom she leads, make two steps slowly backwards, rising on to the ball of the foot which is on the ground. Then, in bending the knees a little, raise again the right foot, which is in front, and glide five short steps backwards on the toes. After which, quitting the hand of he whom she leads, make a curtsy in turning towards the company, and another before him whom she has led.

In this *Bransle* never bend the knees, except, as it were, insensibly on the *pas assemblés*, holding the body and the head firm so as to glide gently to the side. And in order to avoid turning one's back on him whom one leads, a fault common to many, one must carry the toes well outwards, principally that of the right foot.

ON THE FOURTH BRANSLE

THE fourth *Bransle* is named the *Bransle Double de Poitou*, in which we will count fifteen steps in order to make it better understood. The first five are made exactly like the first five of the preceding [*Bransle*], and inasmuch as the

releuer le pied droict qui se trouue deuant, & couler cinq menus pas en reculant sur la pointe des pieds, apres lesquels ayant quitté la main de celuy qu'on meine, faire vne reuerence en se tournant deuant la compagnie, & vne autre deuant celuy qu'on aura mené.

A ce bransle ne faut iamais plier les genoüils, que comme insensiblement aux pas assemblez, tenãt tousiours le corps & la teste ferme, à fin de le couler doucement de costé, & pour empescher de tourner le dos à celuy qu'on meine (deffaut ordinaire à plusieurs) il faut porter les pointes des pieds fort ouuertes, principalement celle du droict.

DV QVATRIESME BRANSLE

LE quatriesme bransle, se nomme le bransle double de Poictou, auquel nous compterons quinze pas à fin de le faire mieux comprendre. Les cinq premiers se font ne plus ne moins comme les cinq premiers du precedant, & parce que les pieds se trouuent ioints ensemble, il faut au sixiesme escarter le pied gauche, à fin d'assembler au septiesme encore vne fois, puis au huictiesme rapporter le pied droict de son costé, en retirant tant soit peu en arriere, & glisser au neufiesme le gauche du mesme costé sur la pointe pour assembler, alors en pliant doucement les genoüils au dixiesme, faut releuer le pied gauche en l'air, qu'on escartera de son costé pour marquer onze, apres lequel faisant porter au douziesme le pied droict deuant quasi à la pointe de l'autre, en dégageant au treziesme le gauche, qui sera glissé à costé, faut que le droict le suiue de prés au quatorziesme, & aussi tost qu'il viendra à se ioindre, on doit escarter le gauche, qui est le quinziesme, & continuer ainsi durant qu'on iouëra l'air.

The METHOD for LADIES

feet are [now] together, for the sixth one must set aside the left foot in order to join [them] once more for the seventh. Then, for the eighth, take the right foot back to the [right] side in withdrawing a very little, and slide the left to the same side on the toe to join it on the ninth. Then gently bending the knees, one must raise the left foot in the air for the tenth, so that it is removed to its own side in order to mark the eleventh. After which, the right foot will be carried in front almost to the toe of the other for the twelfth, disengaging the left, which will slide to the side for the thirteenth. The right must follow it quickly for the fourteenth, and as soon as it comes together, one must set aside the left, which is the fifteenth, and continue thus as long as the air is played.

But it must be observed that on all the *pas assemblés* one must rise, with the toes outwards, without making any movements of the shoulders, inwards or outwards, thus holding the body always straight and level.

ON THE FIFTH BRANSLE

THE fifth is done the same as the preceding one, except that in this, one makes two *glissades* going back to the right side, and in the other one only made one. At the end of which lift up the left foot again, as in the preceding *Bransle*, and, carrying it to the side, make only one *pas coupé* to finish.

As regards the last variation of steps in the *Suite of Bransles*, they are done to the last two couplets of the last of these. On the first of which, scarcely moving from one's place, gently slide the right foot near to the left, rising on to the ball of the feet. Then, instantly letting go the left to the side, and bringing back the other into its place, turn the right shoulder a little outwards, so that the body follows

Mais faut remarquer qu'à tous les pas assemblez, les pointes des pieds ouuertes, il se faut releuer sur icelles sans faire aucun mouuement des espaules en dedans, ny dehors, ains tenir tousiours le corps droict & esgal.

DV CINQVIESME BRANSLE

LE cinquiesme se faict de mesme le precedant, excepté qu'en celuy-cy on fait deux glissades en retrogradant du costé droict, & en l'autre on n'en fait qu'vne, au partir desquelles on releue le pied gauche comme au precedant, & le portant à costé on fait seulement vn pas coupé pour finir.

Pour la derniere diuersité des pas de la suitte des bransles, ils se font sur les deux derniers couplets du dernier d'iceux. Au premier desquels, sans quasi bouger d'vne place, on glisse doucement le pied droict pres du gauche, en se releuant sur le mouuement d'iceux, & à l'instant laschant le gauche à costé, & rapportant l'autre en sa place, on tourne vn peu l'espaule droicte en dehors, que le corps tout d'vne piece doit suiure, puis on faict les mesmes trois pas de l'autre costé, commençant du pied gauche, si bien qu'apres auoir tourné l'espaule gauche en dehors, il faut faire vne retirade du pied droict sans leuer le gauche, que sur le mouuement d'iceluy en pliant vn peu les genoüils, & vne toute semblable de l'autre pied. Puis pliant esgalement les genoüils il faut rapporter le pied gauche en l'air, pour d'iceluy marquer vn pas à costé, qui sera à l'instant suiuy d'vn pas coupé du pied droict.

A ce dernier couplet il faut faire vn temps en coulant lentement le pied droit par dessus le gauche, & vn autre du gauche en le desgageant & portant à costé, puis deux glissades du costé gauche, & deux autres du

all-of-a-piece. Then one makes the same three steps to the other side, commencing with the left foot, so that, after having turned the left shoulder outwards, one should make a *retirade* with the right foot, without raising the left except on to the ball in bending the knees a little; then a similar one with the other foot. Then, bending the knees equally, take back the left foot in the air, to mark with it a step to the side, which will be instantly followed by a *pas coupé* with the right foot.

On this last couplet, one must make a step (*temps*) by sliding the right foot slowly over the left, and another with the left in disengaging it to carry it to the side. Then two others to the left side, and two more to the right side, like unto those of the fifth. So that to finish, it is only necessary to bend the knees gently in order to raise the left foot in the air, which, being carried to the side, will be followed by a *pas coupé*.

ON THE GAVOTTE

AS for the *Gavotte*, which is danced at the end of the *Bransles*, the steps and actions are so common and so well known by everyone, that it will be useless to write of it in detail. Moreover, in many places one dances it diversely, such as in Normandy, where they dance three, of which not only the airs, but the steps and figures are different. And in Flanders, in Artois, and elsewhere, they also dance three altogether different ones, of which the airs, actions, steps and figures bear no resemblance to the aforesaid.

ON THE COURANTE

HAVING considered the diversity of steps in use today in the *Courante*, I found nothing which a Lady may acquire with greater ease, nor which gives her a more

MÉTHODE *pour les* DAMES

costé droit semblables à celles du cinquiesme, si bien que pour finir il ne faut que plier doucement les genoüils pour releuer le pied gauche en l'air, lequel estant porté à costé sera suiuy d'vn pas couppé.

DE LA GAVOTTE

QVAND *à la Gauotte qu'on danse à la fin des bransles, les pas & les actions en sont si communes & si cogneuës de chacun qu'il seroit inutile de la descrire par le menu, d'aillieurs qu'on la danse diuersement en plusieurs lieux, comme en Normandie où on en danse trois, desquelles les airs sont non seulement differents, mais les pas & les figures. Et en Flandre, en Artois, & ailleurs, il s'en danse aussi trois toutes differentes dont les airs, les actions, les pas, & les figures n'ont rien de semblable aux susdites.*

DE LA COVRANTE

APRES *auoir consideré la diuersité des pas de courante qu'on fait auiourd huy, ie n'en ay point trouué qu'vne Dame peust acquerir auec plus de facilité, n'y qui luy donne vne action plus belle ny plus aduantageuse que ceux cy.*

Quand elle aura faict la reuerence comme i'ay enseigné aux bransles, se resouuenant de tenir les pointes des pieds ouuertes, il luy faudra faire porter negligẽment trois pas sans chasser, ny s'esleuer hors terre, mais pliant vn peu les genoüils se releuer sur la pointe du pied qui se trouuera à terre, faisant retirer auec la mesme douceur tant soit peu l'espaule du costé du pied qui aduance, & apres auoir fait chasser le troisiesme, faire vn pas porté & vn pas chassé sur

The METHOD for LADIES

becoming action, neither is more advantageous, than the following.

When she has made the curtsy, as I have taught for the *Bransles*, remembering to hold her toes outwards, she should be made to take three steps negligently, without either a *chassé* or rising off the ground, but bending the knees a little, rise again on to the toe of the foot which is on the ground. With the same softness, draw back the shoulder a very little on the side of the foot which advances. Then, having made a *chassé* for the third, make a *pas porté* and a *pas chassé* first on one and then on the other foot, until the end; on all of which steps the knees must be bent equally, so that the body, very erect, follows the actions of the feet. And take care that the foot which makes a *chassé* is carried level to the side of the foot which is overtaken. Also, in rising off the ground in the *pas porté*, slide the *chassé* softly, falling always on to the toes. She should, nevertheless, keep a somewhat quick measure, without wagging the head, protruding the stomach or bending from the waist, and when bending the knees she should hold the body straight and evenly, without leaning to one side or the other. Moreover, these same steps will be very advantageous for those who, for want of aptitude, are unable to rise off the ground, for if they bend a little low on all steps alike, and rise again on to the toes, they will appear to rise almost as much as those who spring, and with this advantage, that their actions will be much softer. Finally, the master should take care that, according to the nature of those who have a defective figure, it is necessary to make some carry the *pas chassé* in front, in the manner of a *pas coupé*, and others behind, according as to how their defects compel them.

l'vn, puis sur l'autre pied, iusqu'à la fin, sur tous lesquels pas, faut faire plier esgalement les genoüils, à fin que le corps bien droit suiue l'action des pieds, & prendre garde que le pied qui chasse soit porté esgal au costé du chassé, & s'esleuant hors terre sur le pas porté, faut couler doucement le chassé tombant tousiours sur la pointe des pieds, il y faut pourtant obseruer vne mesure vn peu viste sans bransler la teste, aduancer le ventre, ny plier de la ceinture, & en pliant les genoüils tenir le corps droit d'vne façon esgale, sans pancher de costé ny d'autre; au surplus ces mesmes pas seront fort aduantageux pour celles qui manque de disposition, ne peuuent s'esleuer hors terre. Car si elles se plient vn peu bas esgalement sur tous les pas, & se releuent sur la pointe des pieds elles paroistront quasi s'esleuer autant que celles qui saustent, & auec cest aduantage que leurs actions en seront beaucoup plus douces. Au surplus le maistre doit prendre garde que selon la composition de celles qui ont la taille gastee, il est necessaire de faire porter aux vnes le pas chassé deuant en forme d'vn pas couppé, aux autres par derriere, selon que leur deffaut obligera.

DE LA GAILLARDE

IL faut premierement apres auoir esté conduite en presence de la compagnie, faire les deux reuerences qu'on obserue ordinairement aux Gaillardes, de mesme celle dont i'ay cy deuant parlé aux Bransles, & au partir de la derniere continuër le chemin vers le haut bout du lieu où l'on danse, par autant de desmarches que la Musique peut obliger pour prendre la cadence. Puis commencer par vn pas couppé qui se

The METHOD *for* LADIES

ON THE GAILLARDE

FIRSTLY, after having been conducted into the presence of the company, it is necessary to make the two curtsies which are ordinarily observed in the *Gaillardes*, like those of which I have lately spoken in the *Bransles*. Then, in finishing the last, continue the way towards the upper end of the place where one dances by as many steps as the Music obliges, in order to take the cadence. Then begin with a *pas coupé*, which is made with the right foot, after that, bending the knees a little, one must step aside with the right foot in turning the body strongly inwards. After that, rising on to the toes, make the left foot *chassé* nearly to the heel of the right in the air, which must be placed instantly on the ground in relifting the left, with which at the same time one must make a *pas coupé*, such as one does in order to take the cadence. Thus continue on the other foot, without springing or rising off the ground with both feet at once, but softly slide all the steps on the ball of the feet only, and do not bend the knees, except a little at the beginning of all the *five-steps*. And since that every time during the *Gaillarde* one begins the *five-steps* with the left foot one is obliged to turn the body outwards, it is necessary that this be only half done towards the extremities, that is to say, that it is necessary to turn a lot inwards and very little outwards when keeping to the extremities of the room. And, so that the Lady will not inconvenience him with whom she dances, having made a tour of the room with the aforesaid steps, she should stop at either end of the room, and wait till he has finished, in order to make a curtsy to the company, and finish with another to him who will have danced with her.

I would speak of another kind of step which has a graceful air when well performed by a Lady, if the negligence with which one dances a *Gaillarde* today did not prevent me.

fait du pied droict, apres lequel pliant vn peu les genoüils faut faire escarter vn pas du pied droit en tournant fort le corps en dedans, apres lequel s'esleuant sur la pointe des pieds faire que le pied gauche chasse quasi du talon le droit en l'air, qu'il faudra poser à l'instant à terre en releuant le gauche, auec lequel il faut à mesme temps coupper vn pas comme on fait pour prendre la cadence, & ainsi continüer sur l'autre pied sans sauter ou s'esleuer hors terre des deux pieds à la fois, mais couler doucement tous les pas sur le seul mouuement des pieds, & ne plier les genoüils qu'vn peu qu'au commencement de tous les cinq pas, & pource que toutes les fois que durant vne gaillarde on commēce les cinq pas du pied gauche, on est obligé de tourner le corps en dehors, faut que ce ne soit qu'à moitié vers les extremitez, c'est à dire qu'il faut faire tourner beaucoup en dedans & bien peu en dehors tenant les extremitez du lieu, & à fin que la Dame n'incommode celuy auec lequel elle danse, ayant fait vn tour de salle sur les susdits pas, elle doit s'arrester au bout d'ambas, attendant qu'il ait acheué pour faire vne reuerence en presence de la compagnie, & finir d'vne autre deuant celuy qui dansera auec elle.

Ie parlerois d'vne autre sorte de pas qui ont bonne grace estans bien faits par vne Dame, si la negligence qu'on apporte auiourd'huy à danser la Gaillarde ne m'en empeschoit.

Pour clorre donc ce que i'ay entrepris de traitter quand à present sur le suject de ceste Methode, ie conseille à celles qui n'auront pas apris à danser, ou qui pour auoir discōtinué ne se souuiennét plus des obseruations requises à la Gaillarde, de s'en aquitter par la promenade d'vn tour de salle au partir des susdites reuerences, comme pratiquent auiourd'huy plusieurs des mieux dansantes. Car celles-là sont fort

The METHOD *for* LADIES

In order to finish, therefore, that which I have ventured to treat of on the subject of this Method, I counsel those who have not learned to dance, or who from having discontinued, no longer recollect the observances requisite in the *Gaillarde*, to acquit themselves therein, in coming out of the aforesaid curtsies, by a promenade round the room, as is practised today by many of the best danseuses. For those are very culpable who, from timidity or disdain, disoblige those who do them the honour to ask them by [saying] "I do not know how to dance". And although they believe themselves to be honestly excused by these, or such like, words, which without doubt would be becoming, yet if she accepts another for a dance, does not prevent this [plea], or the quality of the excuse given, from being changed into a genuine refusal, thus offending the courtesy of a Gentleman, so that the shame of seeing himself refused would readily make him blush if he had not enough indulgence or was not in the proper humour to turn it all into a jest.

I am content to treat only of such dances as are the most advantageous, of which I have not wished to adorn with a great diversity of steps, although I could have done so. Nay, even of those which the pen appears to find more difficult, since my desire has only been to give a gravity and a modesty that is never to be sought for in the peculiarities and minglings of passages which only have good grace beneath the feet of a juggler. Also, this here is only an essay, which I have resolved to make pleasing before undertaking more, and only await the honour of the commands of those who favour that which I give to the public, in order to treat at greater length upon a subject which these [commands] so justly permit. Also for the ennoblement of other kinds of dances, as much for the satisfaction of the more curious, as for the aid of those who profess to teach them. And, although I make in this, as in all other things, a humble confession of my insufficiency, if I can hope that,

blasmables qui par timidité ou par desdain, desobligent (par vn ie ne sçay pas danser) ceux qui leur font l'honneur de les en prier, & quoy qu'elles croyent en estre honnestement quittes par telles ou semblables paroles, qui sans doute auroient bonne grace, si elles estoient priees de quelque autre danse, ne laissent pas pourtant en celle-cy où la qualité de leur excuse se change en pur refus d'offenser la courtoisie d'vn Caualier que la honte de se veoir refusé feroit volontiers rougir, s'il n'auoit la grace assez asseuree, ou n'estoit d'humeur propre pour tourner le tout en raillerie.

Ie me suis contenté de traicter seulement de ces danses comme les plus vtiles, lesquelles ie n'ay point voulu enrichir d'vne plus grande diuersité de pas, quoy que ie l'eusse peu. Voire mesmes de ceux que la plume semble trouuer plus difficiles, pource que mon desir ne s'estant qu'à donner grauité, & vne modestie qu'on ne doit point rechercher dans la curiosité & meslange des passages, qui n'ont bonne grace que sous les pieds d'vn baladin. Ioint que ce n'est pas icy qu'vn essay que i'ay resolu faire gouster auant que d'entreprendre d'auantage, & n'attens que l'honneur des commandemens de ceux en faueur de qui ie me donne au public, pour traicter plus au long vn sujet que leurs merites authorisent si dignement, & l'annoblir d'autre sorte de danses, tant pour le contentement des plus curieux, que pour le soulagement de ceux qui font profession de les enseigner, & bien que ie face en cela, comme en toute autre chose, vne humble confession de mon insuffisance, si esperay-ie qu'outre que la gloire que ie me suis promise en les obeyssant, me pourroit rendre aysé tout ce que tout le monde pense tenir de l'impossible. Dieu fauorisera mon intention de la grace que ie luy demanderay, qu'il ne refuse iamais aux iustes requestes comme sera la mienne.

The METHOD *for* LADIES

besides the honour to which I am committed in obeying them, I am able to render easy all that everyone thinks to be impossible, God will favour my purpose with his Grace. This I shall ask of him, for he never refuses just requests such as will be mine.

MUSIC FROM HARMONIE UNIVERSELLE

by

MARIN MERSENNE

1636

Transcribed by

EDUARDO M. TORNER

1. Gaillarde

2. Bransle Simple

3. Bransle Gay

4. Bransle à Mener ou de Poitou

5. Bransle Double de Poitou

6. Bransle de Montirande

7. La Gavote

8. Courante

9. Courante à la Reyne

The following music has been included as a matter of interest, although the dances are not described in this book.

10. Passepied de Bretagne

11. Canarie

12. La Bocanne

13. Passamezze

14. Pavanne

15. Allemande

16. Sarabande

17. Volte

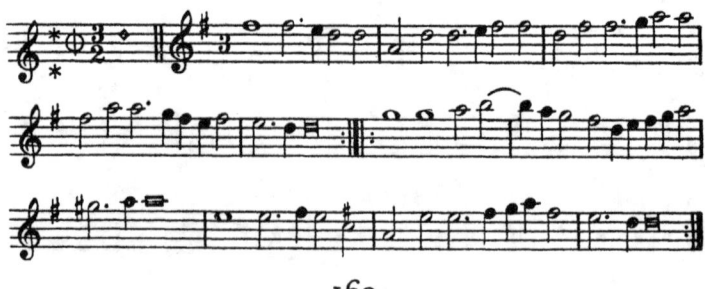

18. La Boëmienne

19. La Moresque

20. Balet

21. Balet

SIMPLIFIED INSTRUCTIONS

Simplified instructions, with notes and comparisons with contemporary documents for

    (A) DEPORTMENT
    (B) DANCING

DEPORTMENT

THE ORDINARY BOW USED WHEN GREETING AN ACQUAINTANCE

First: Remove the hat with the right hand, and take it in front of the "busk of the pourpoint", where it is passed into the left hand, leaving the right hand free.

Advance a few steps until the moment arrives to perform the bow, while looking at the company with a pleasant expression.

The Bow: Having taken the last step on the left foot, pause on it in order to pass the right foot forward in front of the left, so that the legs almost touch as the right passes forward. Without waiting in this position, gently bend both knees outwards, so that they are over the toes, which must be turned out. When straightening the knees, at the finish of the bow, take the weight of the body forward on to the right foot, and at the same time lift the left foot in order to step forward on it, to continue the walk. The body should not be turned, or twisted sideways, for it is sufficient to look towards the person or company to whom the bow is directed.

De Lauze remarks that the same bow should be made "on one foot or the other", according to how the people are

DEPORTMENT

placed. In Rameau's instructions of the Passing Bow, he states that if the persons who are to be saluted are on the right hand of whoever is performing the bow, the right foot should be placed in front of the left, and vice versa.

It will be noticed that in this bow there are no directions for bending the body; in fact, it is to be done "without any gesture or posture of the body". This would agree with the action of the bow as it appears to have been done in parts of mediæval Europe, which was a half-kneel, as may be seen in the genuflexion to the altar today. In this half-kneel, the body is maintained in a natural position, moving only slightly forward as the knees are bent, in order to keep the correct balance of the body.

As De Lauze stresses the importance of turning out the feet both while dancing and when walking, it is quite in keeping that the bow should be performed with the toes and knees outward to each side, and not pointing straight forward.

The style of bowing described by De Lauze shows the gradual transition from the mediæval half-kneel to the action of bowing in later periods, where, by degrees, the body was bent forward more as the legs were kept straighter.

THE BOW BEFORE THE COURANTE

First: Remove the hat with the *left* hand, and hold it "negligently on the thigh". Do not drop the eyes but look straight ahead at the people who are assembled round the room.

The Bow: Keep the weight on the left foot and bend the knees very slightly while carrying the right foot round to the back, placing it obliquely (or diagonally) backward behind the left. The right knee is now straightened, while the left is slowly bent. This bending of the knee *is the bow*. The body is not *bent* forward, it merely

❖ SIMPLIFIED INSTRUCTIONS

inclines slightly over the front leg, while the back is kept straight. On rising from the bow, the left leg is straightened, the body is raised to an upright position, and the right foot is drawn towards the left, on the ball of the foot, until it slides closely behind the left, so that the calves of the legs touch. This completes the first bow, which is directed to the "company".

The Second Bow: The dancer then has to perform the same bow on the other leg to his partner, who is on his right side. To do this, he slightly bends the knees, raising the left foot, which is in front, and pivots a quarter-turn on the right foot, to face his partner, while at the same time the left leg is carried behind, in the same diagonal line behind the right, as in the first bow, with the left knee stretched. The right knee is now slowly bent for the bow, while the body inclines a little forward. He then lowers his head a little to kiss his hand (i.e. his right hand) *before* presenting it to his partner. The left leg is then drawn up behind the right, straightening the body as after the first bow. The Cavalier then faces the front, in order to begin the dance, and replaces his hat on his head.

Every dance was always preceded by two bows, the first being to the company in general, or to the King or most distinguished person present, and the second bow to the dancer's partner. The same two bows were performed after the dance was finished.

It is unlikely that the manner of bowing was identical in all countries, or that each country stuck exclusively to its native fashion. New fashions in manners and dress were foremost among the topics noted, and copied, by travellers to foreign parts.

The Italian Renaissance had, among other things, created a vogue for Italian dancing in France and England

DEPORTMENT

during the fifteenth and sixteenth centuries. Thus it seems that the bows which De Lauze gives for the *dances* were modelled on the Italian method, while those for the ordinary deportment used in saluting a lord or lady were possibly in the French style.

Until well into the eighteenth century the hat was always worn while dancing.

Normally, in the presence of Royalty the hat was held in the hand, but for dancing it was permissible to be "covered", unless a "commoner" happened to be partnering a lady of royal blood.

Pepys records that while the Queen (consort of Charles II) was dancing with the Duke of Monmouth, "who had his hat in his hand", the King came in and kissed the Duke, and *made him put on his hat*, which, as Pepys remarks, "everyone took note of", for indeed it was a significant gesture of Charles towards his illegitimate son.

THE BOW BEFORE THE BRANSLES

The Bow: Step to the side with the left foot, drawing the right back diagonally as for the *Courante*, described above.

Then slide the left foot forward, carrying the weight of the body forward over it, leaving the right foot relaxed behind on the toe. In this position the knees will touch each other. Without pausing here, let both knees bend outward gently over the toes. The body inclines slightly forward, with the weight on the front foot, and when rising from the bow, keep the weight still on the front foot. The back (right) foot is thus released to take a step and the Cavalier kisses his hand as before.

❖ SIMPLIFIED INSTRUCTIONS

THE BOW TO SALUTE A LORD

First: Take off the hat with the right hand, and transfer it into the left, holding it with the inside towards the body, "at the busk of the pourpoint", and walk towards those whom you wish to salute.

The Bow: Slide the right foot forward about the distance of a short step, keeping the legs well stretched and the feet placed with the toes turned outwards. Then bend both knees outward, over the toes, at the same time inclining the body forward from the waist. Do not let the head drop forward, as it only moves in a piece with the whole body. The bow is accompanied by a "gesture" made by sweeping the right hand first forward, and then down towards the ground as the body bends, with the palm of the hand uppermost. The Inferior person might imply by this action that he lays himself at the feet of the Person of Quality. On rising, the right hand is kissed *to* the person to whom the bow is made, after which the arm falls naturally to the side of the body.

(The depth of the inclination for the bow depended on the greater or lesser "quality" of whoever was being honoured. The greater the "quality", the deeper, slower, and more profound was the salutation.)

The bow is finished by moving the left foot, which is behind, to the side, taking the weight of the body on to it. Then slide the right foot behind, relaxing the knee a little, in order to stand easily to converse.

One of the requisites of good deportment, mentioned in the early books of Manners, was a knowledge of how to stand with grace and ease.

It was considered more elegant to place the weight of the body on one foot, as, for instance, Arbeau observes that

DEPORTMENT

statues thus placed look more pleasing than those with the weight equally divided on both feet. The "free" leg was generally slightly in advance of the supporting leg, with the knee relaxed. It is a natural attitude, and one which is shown in most paintings from the sixteenth century onwards.

Therefore one may assume that at the end of the bow, described above, the right foot is brought to the front. With his customary vagueness, De Lauze does not make this clear. It may be that the right foot was kept behind, from whence it could be slid forward, or backward, to perform the slight bows which were obligatory in acknowledging any compliments, with which the conversation of these times abounded.

In 1671, Antoine de Courtin makes the following observations on the manner of saluting "any person of condition. . . . It must", he says, "be done with an humble inflexion of our bodies, taking off our Glove, and putting our hand to the ground" (a later book particularises "the *back* of your hand to the ground"), "but above all we are not to do it precipitously, nor with over much pains, neither throwing ourselves hastily upon our Nose, nor rising up again too suddenly, but gently and by degrees, lest the person saluted, bowing at the same time to you, might have his teeth beaten out by the throwing up of your head."

THE BOW TO SALUTE A LADY

This is performed in exactly the same manner as that for greeting a lord, except that, after kissing his own hand, the Cavalier should then kiss the lady.

The kiss of greeting is of ancient origin, and remained for many years a mode of salutation between men, in all European countries.

❖ SIMPLIFIED INSTRUCTIONS

It seems that, in early days, the practice of kissing in greeting between men and women was more prevalent, and was continued for longer in England than in the southern countries of Europe, where the influence of Eastern thought was stronger.

In Italian and Spanish etiquette, kissing on the cheek, or mouth, in salutation was discountenanced, and it is recorded that when Marie de Medici was betrothed to Henry IV of France, she asked that she might be allowed to follow the custom of her own country, where no woman kissed any man in greeting.

Samuel Kiechel, a merchant of Ulm in Suabia, travelled through most countries of Europe (1585-9). He remarks that in England "when a foreigner, or an inhabitant, goes to a citizen's house as a guest, and having entered therein, he is received by the master of the house, the lady, or the daughter, and by them welcomed—as it is termed in their language—he has even a right to take them by the arm and to kiss them, which is the custom of the country, and if anyone does not do so, it is regarded and imputed as ignorance and ill-breeding on his part: The same custom is also observed in the Netherlands". (From *England as seen by Foreigners in the days of Elizabeth and James I*, by William Brenchley Rye, 1865.)

Antoine de Courtin observes that "if it be a Lady of Quality, we are not to salute her, unless she presents herself in civility, and then only in appearance by putting our faces to her hoods; but whether we salute her or not, our reverence must be performed with a low and decent inclination of the body".

More precise information regarding the etiquette of the kiss of greeting is given by Adam Petrie. Although his book, *Rules of Good Deportment, or Good Breeding*, is dated 1719, he acknowledges that his work is based on the *Rules of Civility*, which was published in the second half of the seventeenth

DEPORTMENT

century. He remarks: "Note that in France they only salute Ladies on the Cheek; but in Britain and Ireland they salute them on the Lips. But Ladies give their Inferiors their Cheek only.... It is Rudeness for a Lady to give her Cheek to her equal, for she should present her Lips."

Numerous references to the kiss of greeting are to be found in the *Diary* of Samuel Pepys. It was the kiss of "civility", or greeting, to which he referred, when he promised his wife that he would restrain his advances to the ladies—"after the first", meaning after the first customary kiss of greeting.

The acts of bowing, kneeling, and kissing in homage undoubtedly originated in primitive society when the subjects, or slaves, grovelled before their kings or masters, prostrating themselves on the ground. Kissing the earth before the superior was part of the abject prostration, unless it was permitted to kiss the feet or the hem of the garment.

To kiss the hand, which did not necessitate a prostration, was a more dignified performance, though this did not supplant the former, for the numerous references to the kiss of etiquette during the sixteenth and seventeenth centuries clearly show that there were varied observances of this custom.

On certain occasions, as when paying respect to Their Majesties at Court, the subject would kiss the hem of the Sovereign's garment, whereas at the same time it was the custom for royalty, or personages of high rank, to greet their subjects, or inferiors, with a kiss.

Their very precise rules of etiquette indicated on what occasions it was correct to kiss the hand of the superior, and when it was requisite to kiss their *own* hand to the person of rank.

In ancient times, customs connected with the religious life of the people were so interwoven with their everyday

SIMPLIFIED INSTRUCTIONS

life, that with such practices as the kissing of one's own hand to another, it is difficult to know which influenced the other. The elaborate ceremonial of kissing of hands and of sacred relics or vessels, in the rites of the Roman Church, corresponds with similar observances of social etiquette of those days.

The kiss of greeting and of homage was certainly an Eastern custom, and the practice of kissing one's own hand to another is a known fashion among the Arabs. An account of Arab salutations, written in the nineteenth century, describes how, when two Arabs clasped hands in greeting, the one of inferior rank could then be allowed to kiss the hand of the superior, but if this concession was prevented by the superior withdrawing his hand, the inferior thereupon kissed his *own* hand to the superior.

The early European books of Courtesy, which were mainly translated from the Italian into other European languages, do not appear to mention this fashion of kissing one's own hand to another. Neither do the books of Etiquette of the eighteenth century. Could it be assumed from this that the fashion was adopted into European usage from the time of the early Renaissance, when Arabian influence was felt in European thought, and which, for a time, became generally adopted?

In the *Refined Courtier* (1663), dedicated by Nathaniel Walker to James, Duke of Monmouth, is found a suggestion of such a possibility. With reference to English modes of greeting is the following passage: "And [they] kiss the hand (*which is no new piece of servility* invented by modern Courtiers, but an exceeding aged solemnity, borrowed from the superstitions of the Ancient Gentiles, who were wont whenever they passed by a Temple or Altar, or saw any creature or Statue in which they imagined a Divinity to dwell) in significance of sacred reverence, to put their hand to their mouth and softly to mouth some petition to

DEPORTMENT

those wooden or stonie Deities, to be propitious to them and prosper their affairs."

It seems strange that in England the memory of this picturesque custom seems to have faded away, for though it may have been observed more on the Continent, it was certainly alluded to in the English deportment books of the seventeenth century, even though these were mostly translated from the French. In the *Rules of Civility* (1685) a gentleman is warned that "it is not improper to advertise that you must always pull off your Glove, and kiss your hand, when you take anything from, or present anything to, a person of Quality, or when you return anything to them: But if he desires you to reach such a thing, you must do it presently [i.e. *at once*] without making him attend [*wait*], and, having presented it, not forget to kiss your hand".

THE PROCEDURE TO BE OBSERVED WHEN ASKING A LADY TO DANCE

First: Take off the hat with the left hand, hold it with the inside towards the body, "on the busk of the pourpoint", and walk towards the lady.

The Bow: Slide the right foot gently in front of the left, and bend both knees outward, over the toes, inclining the body forward as in the bow to salute a lord. The right hand is kissed "in order to take that of the lady". Having done this, the man leads his partner to the "lower" end of the room, which was originally the end facing the King's seat (or "The Presence", as it was called, in later years). This "lower" end of the room was where the musicians were usually placed.

The First Bow before Dancing: This bow is the same as that which has been described for the *Courante*. At the same time that the man bows, his partner makes her curtsy, these reverences being directed to the "com-

pany" before whom they are about to dance, or to the most important person, or personages, present. Kissing his hand again, to retake his partner's, the man leads her to the middle of the room.

The Second Bow before Dancing: It appears that, if among the company there were persons of special importance, who required recognition, these same reverences were then paid to them. Otherwise the couple merely performed their bow and curtsy to each other, in the same manner as the first reverences. After which the man must replace his hat on his head, and if the dance requires that he shall lead the lady by the hand, he will again kiss his hand before offering to take hers.

The Bows at the Finish of the Dance: At the end of their dance, the man and his partner must first perform the bow and curtsy to the company, exactly as they did the first time. They then turn to each other as before, and repeat the salute to each other.

The rigid etiquette of these times was nowhere in greater evidence than in the ballroom.

The ceremony for all balls was modelled on those of the Court, where the King and Queen, or the persons of highest rank present, led, or started, the dancing. At other formal balls, the Master of Ceremonies conducted the proceedings, and arranged the couples according to precedence.

The initial formalities having thus been organised at the outset, the ball progressed tranquilly, unless some unfortunate person, through ignorance or carelessness, upset the routine. Thus, Antoine de Courtin remarks "if a man finds himself by accident surprised in any Assembly, or at a Ball, above all things he is to know exactly, I will not say to Dance, but the rules and formalities of Dancing—for in all Countries they are not the same".

The customary etiquette of Dancing was that the men

DEPORTMENT

and women alternated in taking out their partners, for it was not then the man's sole privilege to seek a partner. The same rule was observed in Rameau's time: "Since", he says, "at all regulated Balls a King and Queen are chosen, it is they who according to rule begin the dancing, and when the first *Menuet* is concluded, the 'Queen' invites another gentleman to come and dance with her, and after they have danced, he takes the Queen back to her place, and politely asks her whom she wishes him to take out...."

THE LADY'S CURTSY

for Receiving, or Meeting, Others in Company

The Curtsy: To perform the curtsy, move one foot (either the right or left) a little to one side, and draw the other foot up gently to join the heels together, with the toes turned out at an angle of about 90 degrees. Do not pause in this position, but immediately let the knees begin to bend, slowly and evenly, taking care to make them go outward, over the toes.

The body does not bend forward, but is held "straight and firm". If the bend of the knees is very deep, the body will naturally *incline* slightly forward in order to maintain the correct balance, but the back must be kept perfectly straight.

The arms should be held away from the body, to each side, with no trace of stiffness.

When bending the knees the eyes should be lowered. If the curtsy is deep the heels must be lifted off the floor, so that the body is balanced on the toes.

As soon as the required depth has been reached, begin to rise again with the same speed and smoothness with which the bend was performed.

On rising, the eyes are again lifted to look at the "company", or person greeted.

✥ SIMPLIFIED INSTRUCTIONS

As in the Cavalier's bow, the depth of the curtsy was regulated by the importance, or "quality", of those present in the company. A curtsy of medium depth was most usual in order to avoid extremes either way.

As the bows and curtsies were a mode of *greeting*, it should be obvious that the important part of the reverence was to *look at* the person to whom the salute was made.

This point should never be neglected by those who portray the manners of bygone days.

De Lauze frequently stresses the importance of directing the gaze to those who are present, either when dancing, or when greeting someone.

THE LADY'S PASSING CURTSY

The Curtsy: The following curtsy is described on the supposition that the person to be saluted is to the right-hand side of the performer.

Step to the side with the left foot, making a quarter-turn to the right, and at the same time slide the right foot gently forward in front of the left, to the distance of a small step.

Bend the knees a little, keeping them over the toes, which are turned outward.

Keep the body perfectly erect, and on rising from the bend, transfer the weight of the body entirely on to the front foot. This leaves the left, or back foot, free to continue walking, and by pivoting a quarter-turn back again to the left while the weight is still on the right foot, the walk can be continued in the original direction.

If those to whom the honour is paid are on the left-hand side, the curtsy is begun by turning on the right foot, making a quarter-turn to the left, and sliding the left foot forward.

DEPORTMENT

In performing this curtsy, the whole body is thus turned squarely to face those who are to be greeted.

When bending the knees keep the weight equally distributed on both feet.

This Passing curtsy was less ceremonial than the preceding one. It could be used on the following occasions:

(*a*) When meeting or passing by people, either out-of-doors or in some large assembly hall.

(*b*) In acknowledging some particular compliment of speech while talking in company.

The more formal curtsy was used in the ballroom for the introductory and parting reverences which were made at the beginning and end of the dance.

❖ SIMPLIFIED INSTRUCTIONS

DANCING

CAPRIOLE

This step may have a remote origin. A similar movement has been noted in the dances of certain primitive tribes in modern times. It seems that among the Angami Nagas "one step in particular which is much practised and admired, consists of a high leap during which there is crossing of the legs three times before the feet again touch the ground". (From J. H. Hutton in *Tribal Dancing and Social Development*, by W. D. Hambly.)

The *capriole* is mentioned in the sixteenth century by both Arbeau and Fabritio Caroso. Arbeau describes it very vaguely, for he merely says: "There are many dancers so agile that, in making the *saut majeur*, they move their legs in the air, and this shaking is called *capriole*." Caroso is much more explicit, and his description corresponds closely with that of De Lauze.

From these two authors we discover that *caprioles* and *entrechats* were steps in which the legs passed, or crossed, each other while springing off the ground. According to Caroso, there were *caprioles* of "three, four, and five" where the legs were passed very quickly in the air these number of times. In the *Capriola Intrecciata*, or interwoven *capriole*, he specifies that the legs were crossed one over the other, being widened sideways between each crossing; therefore it may be that in the ordinary *caprioles* the legs were passed with a forward and backward movement, without actually crossing, and this may have suggested the shaking movement mentioned by Arbeau.

De Lauze's instructions show that the legs were crossed one in front of the other, and anyone who has executed an *entrechat* in ballet will appreciate his advice that if both legs

CEREMONY OF SIGNING A MARRIAGE CONTRACT IN THE KING'S BEDCHAMBER

(*Note division of ladies and gentlemen, and manner of holding hats and fans*)

A MARRIAGE FEAST

(*Showing method of "leading" a lady*)

A YOUNG KNIGHT KISSING HIS HAND AS HE RECEIVES THE ACCOLADE FROM LOUIS XIII

FRENCH NOBILITY

DANCING

are turned outward from the hip, the step will be easier to perform. It would certainly be the case in his day when dancers wore shoes with heels.

Raoul A. Feuillet's book on dance notation was published at the turn of the seventeenth–eighteenth centuries, so that the steps he notated were in use at any rate during the second half of the seventeenth century. The "characters" whereby he distinguishes various *caprioles, demi-caprioles*, and *entrechats* show these crossing movements clearly. In the *entrechats* of 3, 4, 5, and 6 beats, the feet were crossed in the air the corresponding number of times before coming again to the ground. Moreover, the counting of these beats was identical with the manner of counting beats in ballet today, as we can see from the following description of an early eighteenth-century *entrechat*. "As for the Common *Entrechat*, it is performed in the same manner with the Right Caper upon the third position, but in springing you must remember to cross before and behind with your legs *en l'air*, two, three, or four times from the 5th position to the same again. Whereof we distinguish the *Entre-chat* into 3, 4, 5, 6, and 8, because every time that you open your legs in the second position and cross them in the 5th *en l'air* it must be reckon'd for two beatings" (Siris, 1706).

In John Weaver's English translation of the above book of Feuillet's, the *capriole* is translated as *caper*, and in his definition of the steps which were then used in dancing, he says: "Capers are when in rising or leaping from the Ground, one Leg beats against the other, which we call Cutting."

Siris says the same thing in his translation of the same book: "Cutting Capers are when in Springing we beat one leg against the other."

In the sixteenth century it was customary to speak of *cutting* capers, as in *Twelfth Night* Sir Toby Belch asks, "What is thy excellence? in a galliard, Knight?" And

✥ SIMPLIFIED INSTRUCTIONS

Sir Andrew Aguecheek replies, "Faith, I can *cut* a caper".

Caroso proposes the same method of practising these *caprioles* as De Lauze suggests, which is to support the body by the arms, so that the feet, being thus lifted off the ground, may execute the passing and crossing movements more easily. Caroso also makes it perfectly clear that the legs should be well stretched while performing the *capriole*, a point which De Lauze stresses more than once, for he insists that the movement should be taken from the hip.

It may seem surprising to discover that any gentleman of the seventeenth century who "had a figure for dancing high" (otherwise springing), should consider executing a *capriole* of seven or eight beats, for this is judged to be no mean feat in modern ballet. But if one remembers the amazing leaps of certain folk-dancers, as for example the Basques, one may wonder whether these movements were so extraordinary in an age when dancing was an accepted accomplishment.

The Capriole: To perform the step, start with one foot placed just in front of the other, with the toes turned outward (fifth position of the feet in ballet). Spring into the air and beat the legs together and return to the same position, with the same foot in front.

After the beat in the air, the legs could also change places while still in the air, so that on alighting the foot which started in front finishes behind. The step can also be performed alighting on one foot. During this spring the body can turn either a quarter, half, three-quarter, or a full turn while in the air.

Demi-Capriole: A *Demi-Capriole* is described by Siris as a beaten *Jeté*.

In springing forward, the back leg beats in front of the other, after which it receives the weight of the

body. The foot which is now behind is held off the ground, just behind the supporting heel (third position *en l'air*).

Entrechat or *Cross-Caper:* This step was similar to the *caper*, except that when springing into the air the legs were crossed, which meant that they changed places in the air, so that the front leg crossed to the back and then returned to the front before alighting.

PAS COUPÉ

The *coupé* of early days was quite unlike the step which bears this name today. It was called a "compound step" as it consisted of two steps, though as a dance movement it was understood to be but one "pas" or *step*.

In the sixteenth century a *coup-de-pied* was a movement in dancing when, according to Arbeau, "the dancer springs on one foot to support the body, and raises the other forward in the air, as if he wished to kick someone". If the leg was raised high, it was called a *grue*, and if only a small distance from the ground it was named *pied-en-l'air*.

Sometimes in the *Bransles* the ordinary *doubles* or *singles* were "divided" by making these *pieds-en-l'air*. This meant that the *pieds-en-l'air* were inserted in place of some of the slower steps which normally composed the *singles* and *doubles*. When performed thus, the step was known as a *single*, or *double*, "*découpé*"—or "cut up".

The *Bransles* composed in such a manner, of "a medley of *doubles*, *singles*, *pieds-en-l'air*, *pieds-joints*, and *sauts*", were "sometimes varied by the insertion of various slow or quick bars accordingly as it pleases the composers and inventors. Musicians call them *Bransles de Champagne coupés*". Most of these *Bransles Coupés* given by Arbeau contain these *pieds-en-l'air* movements.

Now the characteristic difference between the dancing

SIMPLIFIED INSTRUCTIONS

of the sixteenth and seventeenth centuries was that, throughout the seventeenth century the steps became quieter, that is, they were danced much more smoothly and softly, with gliding and bending steps instead of running and leaping movements. De Lauze bears this out when he says that "these same steps will be very advantageous for those who, for want of aptitude, are unable to rise off the ground, for if they bend a little low on all steps alike, and rise again on to the toes, they will appear to rise almost as much as those who spring, and with this advantage, that their actions will be much softer".

The natural evolution of dance steps from the sixteenth- to seventeenth-century technique would therefore come about through using the same sixteenth-century steps while dancing them in a smooth, gliding manner.

The *pieds-en-l'air* as danced in Arbeau's *Bransles*, and in other dances, were done moving either forward or sideways. If, instead of springing these steps and raising the foot in the air, the steps are danced *terre-à-terre* (i.e. close to the ground), with a soft flexion and extension of the knees and ankles and feet, the movement devolves into a step that is practically the same as the *coupé* as known in the seventeenth and eighteenth centuries.

This is particularly evident when the *pieds-en-l'air* are done to an uneven rhythm, such as the *trochée* (short-long). Mersenne contends that these ancient Greek rhythms were still the basis of the various dance rhythms used in his day.

The name *coupé* may have evolved from the French *coup-de-pied*, or from being connected with the *mouvement decoupé* or *cut-up* steps.

Pas Coupé, as performed forward: Stand on the left foot, with the right foot disengaged behind, on the ball of the foot. Bend both knees outward to each side, at the same time bringing the right foot level with the left, so

DANCING

that the right heel is against the left heel. The right toe is raised so that the foot is parallel with, and does not touch, the ground, while the weight of the body remains on the left foot.

Still keeping the knees bent, carry the right foot forward the length of a short step, then rise on to the ball of the forward foot, straightening the knee. As the knees are stretched the left foot is brought level with the right, and, without pausing, gently passes forward the length of a step, with the toe pointed downward. In taking the weight on to the front (left) foot again, the toe comes to the ground first, after which the heel is gently lowered, "through the foot", to the ground.

ENTRE-COUPÉ

The literal English translation is *intersect*. According to the manner in which De Lauze describes this step, it seems to be a *crossing-coupé*, which was a step very frequently found in the dances of the late seventeenth and eighteenth centuries.

Entre-Coupé: The first step of this *coupé* is performed as described for the forward *coupé*, except that, instead of stepping forward, the step is taken across, either in front of or behind the stationary foot, and the second step is then taken to the side.

PAS ASSEMBLÉ

The meaning of the *pas assemblé* in connection with these dances is to draw one foot up to join the other. It is usually taken from the *second* (feet apart) position of the feet.

❖ SIMPLIFIED INSTRUCTIONS

Pas Assemblé: With the feet in the second position, the knees are slightly bent, in order to give an impetus for the rise on to the ball of one foot while drawing the other foot to join the heels together (in the first position). The weight of the body is thus equally distributed on both feet, while remaining on the toes.

PAS CHASSÉ

The *chassé* is referred to by eighteenth-century masters as the "chasing" or "driving" step, from the fact that one foot "drove" the other by moving into its place, thereby forcing the second step of the *chassé* to be placed either forward, backward, or sideways, according to the direction of the step.

It is not quite clear whether the *chassé* which De Lauze mentions is performed with the legs straight or bent. His instructions to the lady, in dancing the *Courante*, are that she must gently slide the *chassé*, keeping always on her toes, and in the man's *chassé* in the *Courante*, he says, "there should be no bending at the waist, nor should the knees be bent *inwards*". He does not say that the knees should not be *bent*. De Lauze remarks that in the man's *Gaillarde* step, the dancer must "take care not to *chassé* on the toes". It seems likely, therefore, that the step could be performed according to the requirement of the dance, as to whether a springing or gliding movement was used. Possibly what De Lauze calls a *chassé-coulant* was a *chassé* on the toes with stretched legs.

The later Chassé: The manner in which the *chassé* was performed in the late seventeenth and eighteenth centuries was to begin with the feet in the second position (i.e. feet apart) if moving sideways, or in the fourth

DANCING

position (one foot in advance of the other) if moving either forward or backward.

The knees were then bent slightly, outward over the toes, before rising with a slight spring, and in coming again to the ground the "driving" foot fell into the place where the other foot had been, while the latter (i.e. the second step) was placed almost simultaneously either to the side, or forward or backward, according to the desired direction of the step.

Thus, if the *chassé* travelled sideways to the left, the right foot would fall into the place previously occupied by the left foot, "driving" the left foot to the side.

The *chassé* therefore began and finished with the knees bent.

PAS COULER

This "sliding step" was a quick slipping, or running, movement performed on the toes with the legs well stretched. It was probably the forerunner of a step which later English masters called "The Slip before and behind" which was only done moving *sideways*.

The Slip: This Slip step usually consisted of four steps, the first stepping sideways. The second step was then drawn either in front or behind the first, and these two steps were repeated.

The complete step was usually finished by another slow step to the side to which the step travelled.

This complete step corresponds with the sixth, seventh, eighth, ninth, and tenth steps given by De Lauze in the *Bransle de Poitou*, except that he states that the steps are done on the toes, with the legs well stretched, while in the eighteenth-century version the knees were alternately bent and straightened on each movement.

SIMPLIFIED INSTRUCTIONS

PAS GLISSÉ

A *pas glissé*, according to Feuillet, is "when in moving, the foot slides on the ground". Rameau defines the movement as follows: "A sliding step is made by passing the foot gently forwards so that it hardly touches the ground. Hence it must be understood that this step is slower than one in which the foot is moved forwards without touching the ground. Thus a slide implies a very slow step, which contributes in some degree to the perfection of the *coupé*." This means the *second* step of the *coupé*.

A *pas glissé* can therefore be interpreted as a *slow* step in which the moving foot passes lightly over the ground.

GLISSADE

De Lauze uses the term *glissade* to denote a step in the *Bransle* where one foot was placed to the side, after which the other foot was drawn up to join it.

The origin of this step was the mediæval *Simple* or *Single*. When danced in the *Bransles*, the *Single* consisted of a step to the side with one foot, whereupon the other foot was drawn up, closing the feet together.

The term *glissade* is defined later by Rameau as "another kind of *coupé*", which was "used only to move *sideways*".

THE FLEURET

The *fleuret* referred to here is probably the same, or similar to, the step described by Arbeau. It was composed of three steps, the first two being *pieds-en-l'air*, and the last a *grue* (see note on *coupé*). These steps were all done without springing.

In the seventeenth century, when they would be danced in a still more gliding, *terre-à-terre* manner, moving forward,

the step became in time the *fleuret* which was so greatly used in eighteenth-century dances.

RETIRADE

The term *retirade* probably indicated a withdrawing movement.

Retirade: Spring, or rise on to the left toe, raising the right leg, which should be well stretched, to the side. Then bring the leg down, placing the right foot behind the left so that the calves of the legs touch.

It seems that the raised leg was not held any length of time in the air, but was brought down again almost immediately.

THE GAILLARDE

The *Gaillarde* was the dance *par excellence* of the second half of the sixteenth century. It was a dance for a single couple at a time, and after the couple had finished the preliminary bows and curtsies, they either danced round the room together for a few introductory steps, or they straightway began their *Gaillarde* steps, or "passages", which were composed according to their individual tastes. These *passages* were a feature of the *Gaillarde*, and gave the man an opportunity to display his skill, in the manner of a cockbird impressing his mate.

The woman sometimes danced her *passage* first, moving away from the man, who stood and watched her. She could dance either in a straight line to the other end of the room, or in a circle which led her back to where she started from. Then she would stand and watch her partner dance his steps, until he, in his turn, finished in front of her. If the

SIMPLIFIED INSTRUCTIONS

man wished to show off his talent in dancing, he would put in all kinds of intricate steps, such as caprioles, beats, etc.

Juan Fernandez, Spanish Ambassador to England, records that at a Ball at Whitehall Palace on August 19th, 1604, "the Prince" [Prince Henry Frederick, who died in 1612] "was commanded by his parents to dance a *galliard*, and they pointed out to him the lady who was to be his partner; and this he did with much sprightliness and modesty, cutting several capers in the course of the dance—*con algunas cabriolas*". (From *England as seen by Foreigners*, by W. B. Rye.)

There were an infinite variety of set *passages* in the *Gaillarde*. They could also be composed as the dancer wished, but the ordinary *passage* was a set of five steps danced to two bars of music, with three beats in the bar. This became known as the *five-steps*, or *cinque-pas*, sometimes rendered in English as the *sink-a-pace!*

The steps composing the *passages* could be difficult or easy, and danced with high springs, thereby named "dancing high" or *terre-à-terre* (dancing low), which was more suited to the woman's steps. Though the steps might be varied the *passages* obeyed one rule, which was that they must be terminated with a spring into the air on the penultimate note of the music, landing on the ground on the last note, thus marking what Arbeau calls the *cadence*. In a *passage* of *five-steps* which took two bars of triple time, the leap came on the fifth note. If the dancer wished to make a *passage* of *eleven steps*, which took four bars of music, he would not perform the leap until the penultimate note of the fourth bar, this being the eleventh note.

It was, however, much more usual to perform the *passage* of *five-steps*, and this is what De Lauze means when he says: "I counsel such persons" (*i.e. who cannot dance very well*) "when performing the *gaillarde* to abide by the above-named *five-steps*, which done with a becoming grace are

better than a heap of passages that one knows how to do, but which puts one too much in mind of a juggler."

It has been explained elsewhere that the dance technique of the seventeenth century consisted of subdued, gliding movements, as compared with the high springs and leaps of the previous era. Therefore the *five-step* given by De Lauze is a gliding, softly springing step, with a half-turn of the body, first to the right and then to the left, on each *passage*. The dancer, in repeating the passage continuously, would advance up the room in a straight line, providing, as De Lauze says, he took the steps "to the *side*, and not in front" of him.

It appears that a similar manner of dancing the *five-step* was done in Arbeau's time. Among the numerous variations he gives is one which corresponds closely to that described by De Lauze:

"*Another Five-Steps*

"1 *Grue droite*.
2 *Posture droite* without a *petit saut*.
3 *Entretaille gauche* making a *grue droite*.
4 *Grue gauche*.
5 *Saut majeur*.
6 *Posture droite*."

Followed by the Reverse, done on the opposite foot.

The second movement, "*posture droite* without a *petit saut*", is in plain language a step forward, as Arbeau shows in explaining the movement; (the dancers) "instead of placing both feet on the ground for the said *posture*, will support themselves on the heel of the foot in front and hold the knee stiff and not bent".

It is this step which is important, for this manner of performing the *five-step* is carried through to the *pas de gaillarde* of the eighteenth century.

✣ SIMPLIFIED INSTRUCTIONS

Arbeau also shows that in dancing the *five-step*, the dancer could make a half-turn first to the right, and then to the left, in the same manner as in De Lauze's *gaillarde* step. Thus the dancer could move either in a straight line up the room towards his partner, or, if the dancing space was limited, he could move in a circle and "endeavour to finish in front of his damsel".

In his imaginary conversation with Capriole (his supposed pupil), Arbeau says: "In the *Five-Steps* already described, you could replace the *pieds-joints* by *postures*, and further, make the *postures* not forward but sideways, as if you executed a *pieds largis*" (i.e. a step to the side).

Capriole: "Should I always dance my Five-Steps in a straight line when there is room to do so?"

Arbeau: "When I speak of going straight forward, I mean not to turn the body entirely, because you will dance with good grace if you present first your right, then your left side to the damsel, as if you wished to fence. The *grue droite* should show the right side and the *grue gauche* the left side."

These variations could be combined one with another. Although there were many combinations of these *gaillarde* movements, it seems evident that the most usual, basic *five-step* remained essentially the same from the time of Caroso (1581) until the eighteenth century, when it became a step known as the *Pas Tombé and Pas de Gaillarde*.

"Thus, the *pas de gaillarde* is composed of an *assemblé*, a *pas marché* and a *pas tombé*, which is the whole construction and is many times repeated in the dance which bears its name, which inclines me to think that that is the sole reason why it has been given the name *pas de gaillarde*. However it may be, this *pas* is very graceful and justly maintained in use, and is introduced in many ballroom dances. This *pas* can be made *en avant* and *de côté* in the same manner" (Rameau).

The same step appears in the notation of *La Nouvelle Gaillarde* by Pécour, who was a famous dancer and *maître de ballet* of the later seventeenth century.

Although the basic *five-step* originally consisted of five movements, it was not always necessary to execute five movements of the feet, as Arbeau points out: "But you must observe that some *five-steps* are simply called *five-steps* because they occupy the same measure of time as the usual *five-steps*, and yet they may contain more or less than five steps."

Caroso remarks that the name *five-step* is misleading, as there were only two steps. Arbeau gives the tabulation of a *five-step* of three movements and another of two movements. In that of two movements, each step takes one bar of triple time.

According to Mersenne the *gaillarde* step took five measures or bars of triple time, which may have meant that each step could take one bar of music, though the steps fit admirably to two bars of his *gaillarde*.

A Galician folk-dance of today contains a figure known as the *Media Luna* (Half Moon), in which the "step" consists of five movements of the feet, taking two and a half bars of 6/8 time. This figure of the dance is not completed until the "step" has been repeated six times (fifteen bars), with a pause on the last bar, so that the whole figure takes sixteen bars of music, or a strain of eight bars played twice through.

It is most likely that in a *gaillarde* where the dancer made only one movement to a bar, the music would be played faster than for one where the dancer made five movements to two bars, even if occasional very quick steps were interspersed, as in the modern jig.

The speed of the quick *gaillarde* may have been akin to modern 6/4 or 6/8, which gives a two-beat rhythm, and may explain why a *gaillarde* was sometimes in *duple* time.

❖ SIMPLIFIED INSTRUCTIONS

The Five-Step of the Gaillarde: The following directions will be easier to follow if the dancer commences by facing the right side of the room.

1 Bend the knees, taking the R ft. across in front of the L ft., then rise on to the R toe— } *Pas Coupé*
and Take L ft. to the side, stepping on to the toe, then lower the heel.
2 Hop on toe of L ft., making a half-turn to face the left side of the room, bringing R leg to the side of the L, the leg stretched, and the ft. off the floor.
3 Slide R ft. to the side, on the whole ft., taking weight of the body on to it, and remain facing the L side of room.
4 Draw L ft. up to the R ft. (*chassé*), and as it joins the R, take the weight on to the L ft.—and
5 Lift the R ft. in the air, springing into the air at the same time, and immediately lift the L ft. also in the air, so that the feet change scissor-fashion while in the air—and
6 Alight on the R ft.

The step can then be repeated on the other foot. The dancer will now begin the step facing the left side of the room, and on the *hop* will make a half-turn, as before, to face the right side once again.

When the dancer reaches the end of the room, it is necessary, as De Lauze says, to make a full turn on the hop, in order to return down the room.

The man's arm movements which accompany the Five-Step:
1 The arms remain down in a natural position—and } *The Coupé*
2 Raise the arms to each side, not higher than waist-level.

3 Keep the arms raised, or, at the end of the step, begin to lower them a little.
4 On the *chassé*, the arms are lowered until the hands almost touch in front of the body. Do not bend the wrists.
5 On the spring the arms are again raised sideways as before.
6 On alighting, both arms are brought down as for the first step.

De Lauze's counting of the movements is rather confusing as he counts the steps from the *hop*, with the half-turn, but the *coupé* takes up the first beat of the music.

THE COURANTE

At this period there were both ordinary *Courantes* and "figured" *Courantes*, of which the latter had "ses pas mesurez et ses figures particulières". The figured *Courantes* were probably used in the *balets*, where a number of couples danced together.

In the *Courante Reglée* the steps appear to have been arranged according to the fancy of the dancer, or of the master. Good dancers undoubtedly inserted their own steps, as they did in the *Gaillarde*. The sequence of steps given by De Lauze was intended, so he says, as a guide for other masters who might wish to compose their own *courantes*.

De Lauze gives no indication of the pattern, timing, or the co-operation between the man's and the woman's steps. Except for the few introductory steps, he advises the lady to continue throughout with the *pas porté* and *pas chassé*, and remarks that she should "keep a somewhat quick measure, without wagging the head, protruding the stomach or bending from the waist", which does not

SIMPLIFIED INSTRUCTIONS

suggest the slow dance which the *Courante* became towards the later years of the century. The man's steps were more complicated, thus following the style of dancing of the sixteenth century.

In the eighteenth century the *pas de courante* is described by Rameau as a soft spring, or *jeté*, forward on to the ball of one foot, followed by a *coupé* on the other foot. The *jeté*, though it was counted as the first step, was performed on the third beat of the bar, and the *coupé* on the first and second beats.

De Lauze's definition of the step is a *pas porté* and a *pas chassé*, though he says that some people look better if they pass the foot to the front as in a *pas coupé*. As he recommends that the knees should be bent equally on all these steps, it seems evident that the step was performed in much the same manner as Rameau's *pas de courante*.

The man's arm movements, though simple, add to the elegance of the step. On the *jeté* the hands are brought down to meet in front of "the busk of the pourpoint", and on the *Coupé* the hands lift forward, and open a little to each side.

According to Mersenne, each *pas de courante* took one *mesure* (or bar) of triple time, and one could use as many *mesures* as one wished. In other words, the dance could last as long as the dancer wished.

THE BRANSLES

The point of interest here is the information obtained from Arbeau, De Lauze, and Mersenne regarding the *Suite of Bransles*.

Although Arbeau gives twenty-three varieties of the *Bransle* on his *Orchésographie* (1588), he says that it was customary to begin the Ball with a *Suite* of four *Bransles*,

A NOBLEMAN OF LORRAINE BOWING

LADY SNAPPING HER FINGERS IN DANCING

A BOW IN THE ITALIAN STYLE

DANCING

these being the *Bransle Double, Bransle Simple, Bransle Gay,* and *Bransle de Bourgoyne,* followed by others which could be chosen as desired.

Then, in 1623, De Lauze's *Suite* consists of five *Bransles,* which he names the *Bransle Simple, Bransle Gay, Bransle de Poitou, Bransle Double de Poitou,* the "Fifth" *Bransle,* and lastly, the *Gavot* which made the sixth dance in the *Suite.* Although he does not state specifically that the ball was started by dancing *Bransles,* other contemporary sources of information show that this was probable.

Finally, we have Mersenne's *Suite.* Though the date of his book is 1636, he had obtained the King's Privilege in 1629, six years later than the date of De Lauze's book. As the names and the order of the *Bransles* he gives are identical with those of De Lauze (except the fifth, which De Lauze does not name), one may assume that they were speaking of the same dances. He writes: "There are six kinds (of *Bransles*) which are danced now-a-days at the opening of a Ball, one after the other, by as many persons as wish; for the entire company, joining hands, perform with one accord a continual *Bransle,* sometimes forwards, sometimes backwards; it is done with divers movements to which are adapted various kinds of steps, according to the different airs which are used. They dance round very sedately at the beginning of the Ball, all with the same time and movements of the body. The first of which is named the *Bransle Simple* . . . the second is called the *Bransle Gay* . . . the third is named *Bransle-à-Mener,* or *de Poitou* . . . the fourth *Bransle Double de Poitou* . . . the fifth is called *Bransle de Montirande,* and the sixth is *La Gavot.*"

The order of the *Bransles* in the *Suite* is important, for one may thereby ascertain whether the *Suite* retained a definite form in *tempo* (speed) and *time* (changes of time-signature), throughout the years.

Arbeau explains that the dances in his day were divided

into four kinds, as was the case in ancient Greece. These were the *Grave* (slow), the *Gay* (quick), and a combination of the two, *Grave-and-Gay*. The fourth kind, the Pyrrhic, corresponded to such dances as the *Bouffons* (mimetic dances). He then places the *Bransles* in these various categories, and his explanation is that the order of the *Bransles* in the *Suite* was regulated by the persons taking part. The slower *Bransles Double* and *Simple* were danced sedately by the "old people", the quicker *Bransle Gay* by those of the next degree of dignity, the young marrieds, and the *Bransle de Bourgoyne*, seemingly a very quick dance, by the "youngest of all".

The first five *Bransles* in Mersenne's *Suite* follow the same principle, for the *Bransle Simple* was slow, the *Bransle Gay* quicker, the *Bransles de Poitou* and *Double de Poitou* were taken very quickly, and the *Bransle de Montirande* in a very fast *duple* time. The *Gavot* which ended the *Suite* was, however, danced rather slowly.

This slow introduction to Mersenne's and Arbeau's *Suite* resembles the French form of Overture in the seventeenth and eighteenth centuries. "The form of the Overture of Lully's time consisted of a slow Introduction. . . . The distinction between the French and Italian styles, on which so much trouble was expended by the musical writers of the eighteenth century, seems to amount to little more than this; that the French type of Overture began with a slow introductory movement, the Italian type with a quick movement." (Grove's *Dictionary of Music*.)

Although the Round Dance is a world-wide form, it is known that the French have always, to this day, been partial to *Bransles*. Therefore the custom of performing this *Suite* of dances at the beginning of a Ball may easily have influenced composers of this period.

Measures.—Arbeau refers to *mesures* and *rhythms*, saying "some are *duple*, others *triple*". The word *mesure* was used for

what we now call a *bar*, though the French term for *bar* is still *mesure*.

In 1615 Salomon de Caus defines *mesure* thus: "*Mesure* is a certain time by which the notes are measured with raising and lowering the hand. . . . This lowering and lifting is named *Mesure*, of which we have ordinarily two kinds, namely *Mesure Duple*—when the lowering of the hand is equal to its raising—and *Mesure Triple*—when in lowering the hand one holds it down some time before raising it again, in a manner that the time of lowering, the time when it is held down, and the time of raising it are three equal intervals comprised in one *mesure*."

Mersenne agrees with this definition, and states that the terms *binaire* and *ternaire* were used by musicians to denote two beats and three beats in a bar respectively, although he complicates the issue a little by suggesting that these names have been incorrectly used.

Rhythm.—It was Mersenne's opinion that the poets, musicians, and composers of dances and ballets of his own times would benefit by studying the ancient Greek rhythms in order to apply them to the songs and dances which they composed.

He writes at some length on this subject, and includes a "Table of the movements or measured feet" of "Twelve *Mouvemens Simples*" and "Eleven *Mouvemens Composez, de deux et de trois temps, propres pour les Airs et les Dances*". These rhythmic feet are based on the long and short syllables of ancient Greek rhythms.

With regard to their use in song and dance, Mersenne continues: "After having chosen the melody, one must join to it the proper movements, which the Greeks called Rhythm, which is a system composed of different beats (*temps*), according to the subject of which one is dealing. If this movement should be for dances, one must observe the rise and fall, which they name Arsis and Thesis, in order to

❖ SIMPLIFIED INSTRUCTIONS

raise the body on the one, and to lower it on the other, such as they also do when singing, and such as one does again in the *dances de villages*, where those who dance sing at the same time."

Those, he says, who composed music for "*Bransles* and other kinds of fantasies and dances for Ballets", could use many more of these rhythmic movements, because they were not restricted by the words as when composing music for songs.

It was also possible to pass from one kind of rhythmic movement to another, as for example, from the Spondee (long, long) or the Dactyl (long, short, short), which the musicians of his day called *mesure binaire*, to that of the Iambic (short, long) or Trochee (long, short) which they named *mesure ternaire*. ("*Par exemple—l'on peut passer du Spondaique, ou Dactylique, à l'Iambique, ou Trochaique; ce que les Patriciens appellent passer de la mesure binaire à la ternaire.*")

To quote Grove's *Dictionary of Music*, a foot in music "is a uniform combination of time-units independent of 'time', and a bar a uniform division of time regardless of the particular time-units it contains". Therefore these rhythmic feet were probably not always confined within the bars, as for instance, in the *Bransle Gay*, where the rhythm is given as *short, short, long, long* for two bars of triple time, and in the *Bransle de Poitou* when the rhythm is counted in five beats whilst the measure is triple. (See *Bransles Gay* and *de Poitou*.)

Mouvemens.—Like so many theorists of those days, Mersenne's phraseology is sometimes confusing. It seems that he uses the term *temps* to denote the single beats in a measure or bar, while the word *mouvemen* is used to express the beats of which the rhythmic feet are composed. Therefore, when the rhythmic feet are combined with the measures of duple or triple time the terms *temps* and *mouvemens* appear to denote the same thing, the only

DANCING

difference being that the first is regulated to the bar, whereas the second is not. Thus six bars of *binaire* (duple) time contain, according to Mersenne, twelve *mouvemens*, and two bars of *ternaire* (triple) time have six *mouvemens*. This same rule is applied consistently throughout the *Suite of Bransles*.

Steps (Pas).—As all the *bransles* in the *Suite* are in either duple or triple time, it seems that the rhythms Mersenne gives were for the steps, for the rhythm of each *bransle* is completely different. He says, in fact, "With regard to these movements which they join to the melody, they have no other rules than the steps under which they are performed, as one can see in the examples of dances that I have made . . . where I have tried to relate them with certain movements, leaving every one free to reduce them to any such other feet, or movements, that they may deem correct".

The Suite of Bransles.—In describing the *Suite of Bransles*, Mersenne gives the number of bars, steps, and *mouvemens*. He also gives the rhythm as expressed in Greek rhythmic feet, and states whether the time is duple or triple.

In the following table the terms Duple and Triple are used as by Arbeau and Mersenne.

Arbeau's Suite (1588)

1. *Bransle Double*	Grave-and-Gay	Duple time
2. *Bransle Simple*	Same	Duple time
3. *Bransle Gay*	Quicker	Triple time
4. *Bransle de Bourgoyne*	Very quick	Duple time

De Lauze's and Mersenne's Suite (1623–29/36)

1. *Bransle Simple*	Slow	Duple time
2. *Bransle Gay*	Quicker	Triple time
3. *Bransle de Poitou*	Quicker still	Triple time
4. *Bransle Double de Poitou*	Very quick	Triple time
5. *Bransle de Montirande*	Very fast	Duple time
6. *La Gavot*	Rather slower	Duple time

✥ SIMPLIFIED INSTRUCTIONS

The information compiled from Arbeau, De Lauze, and Mersenne makes the following points evident:

1. That the Ball was opened by the whole company dancing the *Bransle* together.
2. That these *Bransles* were arranged in a *Suite* which kept the same order.
3. That the first *Bransles* in the *Suite* were slow, and the succeeding ones increased in speed until the last, which returned to a slower tempo.
4. That the *Suite* commenced in duple time, the middle *Bransles* being in triple time, and, in Mersenne's time, finished in duple time.

THE FIRST BRANSLE

The *Bransle* was performed by a line of people holding hands, generally in circle formation.

As the name implies, a feature of the dance was the swaying effect caused by the steps being danced first to one side and then to the other. This "return movement" rather resembles what has been called the Pilgrim Step, which is of very ancient origin and which was used in sacred processional dances. In the Pilgrim Step the dancers moved forward and backward instead of from side to side, but it is possible there may have been some connection between the two.

The steps performed to the left side were made with a longer stride than those to the right, as this enabled the dancers to achieve a gradual left-ward course round the room, which was the rule in the *Bransle*. As in normal society the participants usually faced inwards, it followed that the circle of dancers moved in a clockwise direction, or "with the sun". The witches, when performing their sinister dances, were known to face outward on occasions, which would cause the circle to move against the sun . . . widdershins.

The steps of the *Bransle Simple*, as notated by Arbeau, show a marked resemblance to those described here by De Lauze.

DANCING

The ordinary method, according to Arbeau, was to dance a *double* to the left and a *single* to the right, but it is obvious from a perusal of the numerous *Bransles* recorded by him that the fashion of using *pieds-en-l'air* in place of the slower *doubles* and *singles* had become popular. "Young men who have an excess of agility", he observes, "make these divisions at their pleasure. But I counsel you to dance them sedately."

Arbeau therefore gives an alternative example in which this *mouvement decoupé* can be used in the *Bransle Simple*. Executed in this manner, the steps moved only to the left, and consisted of a sequence of seven movements of the feet and a pause on the eighth beat.

The *Bransle Simple* which De Lauze describes, contains eight steps, moving to the left. I offer the opinion that the last three steps (numbers six, seven, and eight) developed from the *pieds-en-l'air* which constituted the *single decoupé* at the end of Arbeau's *Bransle Simple*, and that the rise on to the ball of the foot in De Lauze's *Bransle* was substituted for the springing movements. Even Arbeau advises that the *decoupé* should be danced "sedately". Mersenne gives ten steps for the *Bransle Simple*, though he says that originally there had been eight.

Both Arbeau and Mersenne give six bars of "duple" time (two beats in a bar) for this sequence of steps. The following tables may help to show the similarity between the early and later *Bransle Simple*.

Arbeau (1588)

Bars	Beats		
1	1	Step to side with L ft.	
	2		
2	1	Draw R ft. to L ft.	These four steps make a *double* to the left.
	2		
3	1	Step to side with L ft.	
	2		
4	1	Close R ft. to L ft.	
	2		

❖ SIMPLIFIED INSTRUCTIONS

Bars Beats

5 { 1 *Pied-en-l'air* with L ft.   }
    { 2 *Pied-en-l'air* with R ft. } These three steps make a
6 { 1 *Pied-en-l'air* with L ft. } *single decoupé* (to the left).
    { 2 Rest }

De Lauze and Mersenne (1623–29/36)

In addition to the number of bars and beats in the music, Mersenne gives the rhythm as *long, short, short, long, long*. In order to give the correct interpretation of the speed of the music according to our modern understanding of the note values, it has been transcribed by Professor Torner in *common time*. Thus the following sequence takes three bars of four counts instead of the six bars of two counts as described by Mersenne. Also as De Lauze's sequence consists of eight steps, not ten, the rhythm has been adapted as follows:

Bars Beats   *Rhythm*

1   1   *First Step:* Take the L ft. forward and outward to the side, so that it describes a semi-circle in moving, with the toe turned well out, and step on to the whole foot. The   *Long*

     2   whole body, including the head, turns a little to the left, to follow the direction of the leg.

     3   *Second Step:* Slide the R ft. in front of the L, so that the R heel is placed in front of the L toe. The legs are straight, and the body and head remain turned to the L as above, though the R shoulder is kept back so that the dancer does not turn his, or her, back on the person they lead.   *Short*

     4   *Third Step:* Carry the L ft. to the side again, the length of half a foot, while turning the body back again in order to look straight in front. All these steps are done on the whole foot.   *Short*

DANCING

Bars	Beats		Rhythm
2	1	*Fourth Step:* Draw the R heel to join the L heel, while rising gently "all of a piece" on to the ball of the foot, keeping the legs straight. The body and head remain facing	Long
	2	the front.	
	3	*Fifth Step:* Carry the L ft. gently to the side, the length of a half-foot, remaining up on the toes, the legs straight. Theoretically the body and head remain facing the front, but in practice they begin to turn slightly to the right in anticipation of the next	Long
	4	(sixth) step.	
3	1	*Sixth Step:* Slide the R ft. behind the L heel on the ball of the foot, while letting the body and head turn "all in a piece" a little	Long
	2	to the right.	
	3	*Seventh Step:* The fact that the R ft. is crossed behind the L, and the body turned a little to the right, causes the L ft. to describe a half-circular movement *in the air* outward to the left for the next step. In performing this movement make a very slight rise on to the ball of the R (back) ft. as the L ft. sweeps outward, and step to the side on to the L toe, allowing the body and head to return again to face the front.	Short
	4	*Eighth Step:* Take the R ft., with the toe pointed downward, across to the toe of the L ft., allowing the weight of the body to be taken on to the toe first, and then let the heel come gently to the ground. The L ft. remains behind on the ball of the foot.	Short

SIMPLIFIED INSTRUCTIONS

THE SECOND BRANSLE

Here again there is a similarity between the *Bransle Gay* of Arbeau and that of De Lauze.

Arbeau's version consists of *four steps*, danced always to the left, to two bars of triple time (three beats in a bar). The steps are composed entirely of *pieds-en-l'air*, and would therefore be performed more naturally on the toes.

De Lauze's *Bransle* is also composed of *four steps*, moving to the left, and performed almost entirely on the toes. Mersenne likewise gives the music as two bars of triple time (three beats in a bar), though it is here transcribed with six beats to the bar; hence in the second example the sequence takes only one bar. The rhythm given by Mersenne is *short-short-long-long*.

Arbeau (1588)

Bars   Beats

1
- 1 Step sideways *on to* L ft., making a *pied-en-l'air* right.
- 2 Bring R ft. up to L, and *place it on ground*, making a *pied-en-l'air* left.
- 3 Step sideways *on to* L ft., making a *pied-en-l'air* right.

2
- 1 Bring R ft. to L ft. and *place it on ground*, making a *pied-en-l'air* left, and hold it.
- 2 } Pause.
- 3 }

De Lauze and Mersenne (1623-29/36)

In the following the movement is taken from the hips and the insteps, the knees only bending as a preparation for the *pas assemblés*. The head should not be turned, except with the body, "all in one piece".

DANCING

Bars	Beats		Rhythm
1	3	*First Step:* Before taking the first step, rise on to the toes, the heels touching. Then step to the left on the ball of the foot.	Short
	and	*Second Step:* Join R ft. to L ft. with heels touching, keeping up on the toes. As a variation this step could be placed behind the L ft., in which case the body and head should turn slightly to the right.	Short
	1	Pass the L ft. gently to the side with the toe raised from the ground, the heel of the R ft. being lowered to the floor, while the right knee begins to bend slightly (*Pas Glissé*).	Long
	and		
	2	*Third Step:* Step on to the L ft. to the side, the knees being bent.	Long
	and	*Fourth Step:* Draw R ft. up to L ft., with the heels together, while rising on to the toes and stretching the knees (*Pas Assemblé*).	

THE THIRD BRANSLE

This *Bransle* could be considered the climax of the *Suite*, for here each dancer had a part to play on his own. The dancing-masters of the eighteenth century assert that the *Minuet* was originally derived from the *Bransles of Poitou* and *Anjou*.

Arbeau and Mersenne are in agreement again regarding the music, both giving a phrase of six bars of triple time (three beats in a bar). "Its measure", says Mersenne, "is *sesquialtere*, or *hemiola*", both of which were a species of quick three-time. Having said this, he adds that "its measure is *peonique*", which is the term he uses for a five-beat rhythm. As the music of his *Bransle de Poitou* does not lend itself to a five-beat rhythm, Mersenne may have been alluding here to the measure, or rhythm, of the *steps*. The steps of this *Bransle* fit very well to a five-beat rhythm, and

✤ SIMPLIFIED INSTRUCTIONS

particularly to that of the first *peonique* followed by the fourth *peonique* (*short, short, short, long; long, short, short, short*), and again the first *short, short, short, long*.

If this rhythm is fitted exactly to a phrase of six bars, it follows that the two *long* beats must stand for three beats instead of the normal two beats. When danced in this way, it will be found that the rhythm of the steps is very similar to the notes of Arbeau's *Bransle de Poitou* in his *Orchésographie*.

On the other hand, if Mersenne intended that the steps should be counted in a true five-beat rhythm, the *long* beats would stand for two beats each. It is quite easy to dance the steps in this way, which means that the completed "step" takes *five* bars instead of six, and it requires to be danced six times through in order to begin again on the first bar of the phrase on the seventh time. The phrase of six bars must be played *five* times through to accomplish this.

In the notation of this *Bransle* the steps have been set down both ways; the first to six bars, and the second to five.

The *Bransle de Poitou* was apparently a chain-dance which wound about the room in a serpentine figure. According to Mersenne it was commenced by the man whose duty it was to begin in releasing the hand of the lady on his left, and making a bow to the lady on his right side. Then, "kissing the hand", he retook the hand of the lady on his right, whereupon he began the dance, turning in front of his partner, who followed him, so that they both continued to dance down the line of dancers, who were now face to face with them. During this "inward" turn of the figure it seems that the leader held the partner's hand on the waist, at the side, but that on the "outward" turn they opened the arms so as to "lead with greater freedom".

"This *Bransle*", says Mersenne, "is called *Bransle à Mener*, or *de Poitou*", and the fact that he states "now each leads the *Bransle* in his turn", infers that each person probably

led the whole line of dancers, and not merely his own partner. Mersenne continues: "And having made *one or two turns about the room*, he leaves the lady, whom he held by the hand, in order to find the tail of the *Bransle*, and gives his left hand to the lady whom he finds at the end."

From De Lauze's instructions it seems that as soon as the leader reached the last dancer in the line, he turned off round to his left, and continued back again round the room on almost the same track. This would mean that the leaders, and those following who turned thus to the left, would then be dancing back to back with the remaining line of dancers, so that the general effect would be that of a snaking, serpentine movement.

Then, having returned, as De Lauze says, "to the place whence you started", the leader again turned round in front of his partner (the lady on his right), as he did in the first instance, with a few dancing steps and *pas assemblés*, which he used as a means of "retiring" from the lady he had led. Thus the dancers would have completed a full figure eight from the start to finish of the movement, which bears out the remark in *The Malcontent* by John Marston (1604), that the *Bransle* was "but a figure eight". It is also interesting in that the original form of the *Minuet* was said to be a figure eight, becoming later a S formation, which was finally changed by Pécour to a Z.

It seems apparent that, the leading man having bowed himself away from his position at the head of the line, the whole proceeding was then repeated by his partner, the leading lady. Thus interpreted, De Lauze's instructions become more lucid. It is obvious that the *couple* do not retire to the end of the line together, for the man is told that he "must let her go, *after* having turned on the left hand to take the same course again", which he follows in order that he may arrive back at the place whence he started, where he dances some steps before *leaving* the lady. By doing this

❖ SIMPLIFIED INSTRUCTIONS

the man returns his partner to the head of the *Bransle* again, from whence she can lead in her turn. This explains De Lauze's directions to the lady, which include references to "the one whom she has led", as in the final leave-taking where she was admonished to make the usual two curtsies, the first being, as etiquette demanded, to the "company", while the second was directed to "he whom she had led", and not to the partner who had *led her*.

This manner of leading by turns would be in accordance with the custom of these times, when the men and women alternated in "taking out" their partners.

The steps, performed on the toes with the legs well stretched, were danced at a swift pace according to Mersenne: "Le *Bransle* qui coule fort viste." He gives the number of steps in the sequence as being nine. De Lauze asserts that the "common" *Bransle de Poitou* has "only ten steps but to make it understood with less difficulty we will count twelve". This suggests the use of *compound steps* such as the *coupé*. In the *Fifth Bransle* he uses this term, remarking that the dance finished with *only one pas coupé*, thus justifying the assumption that the last four steps in both the third and fourth *bransles* formed two *pas coupés*. The *Bransle de Poitou* would consequently consist of ten steps, and if step numbers three and four are also rendered as one *coupé*, the number is reduced to the nine cited by Mersenne.

When a *coupé* was performed in three-time, the customary rule was that the first step took up the first beat of the music, and the second step, which was slower, the second and third beats. This rule has been followed where possible in those *Bransles* which are in *triple time*.

After the bow and curtsy, the leader turned in front of the person on his or her right by dancing "one or more *pas couler*", this *entrée* being finished by a step to the left so that the feet were apart about the distance of a short

DANCING

step. From here the steps of this *Bransle* commenced as follows:

Bars	Beats		Rhythm
1	1	*First Step:* Bend the knees slightly as an impetus to draw the R heel up to the L heel, rising on to the toes, the legs well stretched.	Short
	2	*Second Step:* Step to the left on L toe.	Short
	3	*Third Step:* Place R ft. in front of L ft., remaining on the toes.	Short
2	1, 2, 3	*Fourth Step:* Slide L ft. gently to the side on the toe, taking the weight on to the toe first, and probably allowing the heel to sink to the floor.	Long
3	1, 2, 3	*Fifth Step:* Bend the knees slightly and draw R ft. to L ft., rising on to the toes so that the heels touch (*Pas Assemblé*).	Long
4	1	*Sixth Step:* Step to the side on L toe, the legs well stretched.	Short
	2	*Seventh Step:* Place R ft. in front of L ft. on the toes.	Short
	3	*Eighth Step:* Step to side again on the L toe.	Short
5	1	*Ninth Step:* Place R ft. in front of L ft. on the toe. } *Pas Coupé*	Short
	2	*Tenth Step:* Slide L ft. gently to the side on the toe, and probably let	Short
	3	heel come to the floor.	Short
6	1	*Eleventh Step:* Draw R ft. to the L ft., rising on the toes. } *Pas Coupé*	Long
	2	*Twelfth Step:* Slide L ft. gently to the side and allow heel to come to the	
	3	floor.	

✤ SIMPLIFIED INSTRUCTIONS

The leave-taking movements, if continued to the same rhythm, may have been performed somewhat in this manner:

Bars	Beats		Rhythm
1	1	Draw R ft. to the L ft. as for the first step.	Short
	2	Slide L ft. to the side, turning in front of the	Short
	3	partner who is on the right.	Short
2	1	Take a slow step backward with the R ft.	Long
	2		
	3		
3	1	Take a slow step backward with the L ft.,	Long
	2	rising on to the ball of the foot.	
	3		
4	1	Tiny step back on the R ft. on the toe.	Short
	2	Tiny step back on the L ft. on the toe.	Short
	3	Tiny step back on the R ft. on the toe.	Short
5	1	Tiny step back on the L ft. on the toe.	Short
	2	Tiny step back on the R ft. on the toe and let go of the hand of the one you are leading,	Short
	3	and begin the bow to the "company", and	Short
6	1	then bow or curtsy to the person you have led.	Long
	2		
	3		

Whereupon the leader leaves the head of the line, and places himself or herself at the end, giving the left hand to the right hand of the last dancer.

DANCING

The pattern made by the *Bransle de Poitou*:

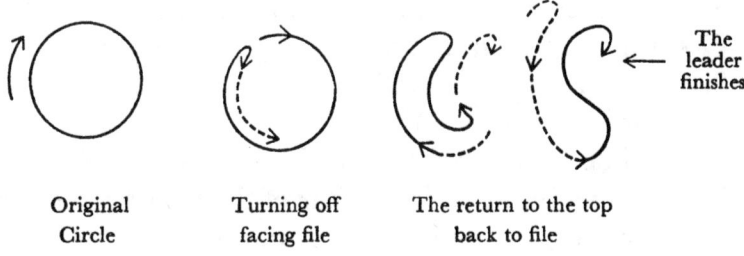

Original   Turning off   The return to the top
Circle   facing file   back to file

(The plain line denotes the file of dancers)

The same steps arranged to five-beat rhythm.

Bars	Beats		Rhythm
1	1	*First Step:* R ft.	Short
	2	*Second Step:* L ft.	Short
	3	*Third Step:* R ft.	Short
2	1	*Fourth Step:* L ft.	Long
	2		
3	3	*Fifth Step:* R ft.	Long
	1		
	2	*Sixth Step:* L ft.	Short
	3	*Seventh Step:* R ft.	Short
4	1	*Eighth Step:* L ft.	Short
	2	*Ninth Step:* R ft. ⎫ *Coupé*	Short
	3	*Tenth Step:* L ft. ⎭	Short
	1	*Eleventh Step:* R ft. ⎫	Short
5	2	*Twelfth Step:* L ft. ⎬ *Coupé*	Long
	3	⎭	
6		Repeat from beginning.	

❖ SIMPLIFIED INSTRUCTIONS

In Mersenne's *Bransle de Poitou* the first six bars are repeated, and then the next twelve are repeated; therefore, when the complete step is danced to five bars it will recommence each time on the following bars:

First time begin on first bar.
Second time begin on sixth bar.
(Repeat these six bars.)
Third time begin on fifth bar of first repeat.
Fourth time begin on fourth bar of the next twelve bars.
Fifth time begin on ninth bar of the same.
(Repeat these twelve bars.)
Sixth time begin on second bar of second repeat.

Leave-taking begins on seventh bar of same. Bow on last bar of same.

THE FOURTH BRANSLE

As soon as each dancer had in turn led the previous *Bransle*, the company formed a circle in order to continue the remainder of the *Suite*. "Et si tost que chacun a mené quelqu'un a son tour, on se remet en rond pour dancer les autres *Bransles*." So writes Mersenne, though De Lauze affirms that these last dances were very little used, people amusing themselves more in entertainment than in dancing seriously. It can be imagined that the irregularity and lively pace of the *Bransle de Poitou* had the effect of breaking up the steady continuity of the preceding dances.

De Lauze enumerates fifteen steps for this *Bransle Double de Poitou* "in order to make it understood with less trouble", while Mersenne says there are eleven steps to eight bars of music, which is still in triple time, but with a changed rhythm of *short-long*. If it can be assumed that the third and fourth steps, the twelfth and thirteenth steps, and the fourteenth and fifteenth steps compose three *pas coupés*, as in the third *Bransle*, this *Bransle* can be said to contain eleven steps, as the tenth is not an actual *step*.

DANCING

Bars	Beats		Rhythm
1	1	*First Step:* Bend the knees slightly, and draw the R ft. to the L ft., rising on to the toes.	*Short*
	2	*Second Step:* Step to the side on the L ft. on the toe.	*Long*
	3		
2	1	*Third Step:* Place R ft. in front of L ft. on the toe.	*Short*
	2	*Fourth Step:* Slide L ft. gently to the side, the toe pointed and allow heel to come to the ground. *Pas Coupé*	*Long*
	3		
3	1	*Fifth Step:* Bend the knees and draw R ft. to L ft. as in the first step (*Pas Assemblé*).	*Short*
	2		*Long*
	3		
4	1	*Sixth Step:* Step to the side on L ft.	*Short*
	2	*Seventh Step:* Draw R ft. to L ft. without taking the weight on to the foot (*Glissade* to left).	*Long*
	3		
5	1	*Eighth Step:* Step to the R with R ft.	*Short*
	2	*Ninth Step:* Draw L ft. to R ft. without taking the weight on to it (*Glissade* to right).	*Long*
	3	*Tenth Step:* Lift L ft. in the air.	
6	1	*Eleventh Step:* Step to the side on to L ft.	*Short*
	2		*Long*
	3		
7	1	*Twelfth Step:* Place R ft. to the toe of L ft.	*Short*
	2	*Thirteenth Step:* Slide L ft. gently to the side. *Pas Coupé*	*Long*
	3		
8	1	*Fourteenth Step:* Join the R ft. to L ft. *Pas Coupé*	*Short*
	2	*Fifteenth Step:* Take L ft. gently to the side.	*Long*
	3		

❖ SIMPLIFIED INSTRUCTIONS

THE FIFTH BRANSLE

Mersenne names the Fifth the *Bransle de Montirande*. It consists, he says, of three separate parts, each part being composed of a different number and composition of steps, and set to a phrase of eight bars. "Sa mesure", he observes, "est binaire, mais elle est forte viste", the rhythm being *short-short-long*.

This appears to conform with the information gleaned from De Lauze, who intimates that this *Bransle* has three couplets, while the steps defined by him fit very well to the phrases of eight bars. Dancing-masters used the term *couplet* to denote a figure of a dance which could contain anything from about six to sixteen or more bars of music.

The steps of the first *couplet* of eight bars are practically the same as those of the *Fourth Bransle*, except that there are two *glissades* to the right instead of one, and it finishes with only one *pas coupé* to the left.

The First Couplet

Bars	Beats		Rhythm
1	1	Bend the knees slightly and draw R ft. to L ft.,	Short
	2	rising on the toes.	
	3	Slide the L ft. to the side on the toe.	Short
	4		
2	1	Place R ft. in front of L ft. on the ⎫	Long
	2	toes. ⎪ *Pas Coupé*	
	3	Slide L ft. gently to side on the toe, ⎬	
		and let heel come to the ground. ⎪	
	4	⎭	
3	1	Bend the knees and draw R ft. to L ft., rising	Short
	2	on the toes (*Pas Assemblé*)	
	3		Short
	4		

DANCING

Bars	Beats		Rhythm
4	1 2 3 4	Step to the side on L ft. Draw R ft. to L ft. without taking the weight on it (*Glissade*).	*Long*
5	1 2 3 4	Step to right on R ft. ⎫ ⎬ *Glissade* to right Close L ft. to R ft. ⎭	*Short* *Short*
6	1 2 3 4	Step to right on R ft. ⎫ ⎬ *Glissade* Draw L ft. to R ft. without taking ⎬ to right weight on to it. ⎭	*Long*
7	1 2 3 4	Bend the knees and lift the L ft. in the air and— Step on it to the left.	*Short* *Short*
8	1 2 3 4	Place R ft. to the toe of L ft. ⎫ ⎬ *Pas* Slide L ft. gently to the side, toe ⎬ *Coupé* pointed down, and let heel come to the ground. ⎭	*Long*

The Second Couplet

1	1 2 3 4	Join the R heel to the L, rising on to the toes, and, hardly moving from the spot, take a step to the side on L ft. ⎫⎬⎭	During these three steps, which constitutes a kind of *chassé*, the body is turned all in one piece to the R, thus making a small quarter-circle to the left with the feet.	*Short* *Short*
2	1 2 3 4	Close the R ft. again to the L ft., which releases the L ft. to the side. ⎫⎬⎭		*Long*

213

SIMPLIFIED INSTRUCTIONS

Bars	Beats			Rhythm
3	1	Join the L heel to the	During these three	Short
	2	R on the toes.	steps the body	
	3	Step to the right with	turns back again	Short
	4	R ft.	to the L, while the	
4	1	Close the L ft. to the	feet move to the	Long
	2	R ft. keeping on	right, thus com-	
	3	the toes.	pleting a small half-	
	4		moon.	
5	1	Raise the R ft. to the side, rising, or	Retirade with R ft.	Short
	2	springing on the L toe.		
	3	Place the R ft. behind the L ft.		Short
	4			
6	1	Raise the L ft. to the side, rising or	Retirade with L ft.	Long
	2	springing on the R toe.		
	3	Place the L ft. behind the R ft.		
	4			
7	1	Bend the knees and lift the L ft. to the side in		Short
	2	the air.		
	3	Step to the side on L ft.		Short
	4			
8	1	Place R ft. in front of L toe.		Long
	2		Pas Coupé	
	3	Slide L ft. to the side on the toe, and allow the heel to come to the ground.		
	4			

The Third Couplet

			Rhythm
1	1		Short
	2	Slowly slide the R ft. across in front of the	
	3	L ft. and step on to it.	Short
	4		
2	1	Disengage the L ft., pointing it to the side,	Long
	2	with no weight on it.	
	3		
	4		

DANCING

Bars	Beats		Rhythm
3	1 Step to the left on L ft. 2 3 Close R ft. to L ft. 4	Glissade to left	Short Short
4	1 Step to the left on L ft. 2 3 Draw R ft. to L ft. without 4 taking the weight on to it.	Glissade to left	Long
5	1 Step to the right on R ft. 2 3 Close L ft. to R ft. 4	Glissade to right	Short Short
6	1 Step to the right on R ft. 2 3 Draw L ft. to R ft. without 4 taking weight on to it.	Glissade to right	Long
7	1 Bend the knees, lifting the L ft. to the side in 2 the air and 3 Step on it to the side. 4		Short Short
8	1 Place R ft. to the toe of L ft., on the toes. 2 3 Slide L ft. to the side, the toe pointed down, 4 and let the heel come to the ground.		Long

As De Lauze gives no information regarding the *tempo* or *rhythm* of the steps, I have had to use my discretion in arranging these to agree with the music and rhythm set by Mersenne.

In doing this I have, for instance, paid attention to the manner in which De Lauze describes each step, assuming that when he remarks "without pausing on this" he is probably speaking of a *short* or *quick* step, while another

SIMPLIFIED INSTRUCTIONS

which he specifies as "sliding gently" indicates a *long* or *slow* step.

Although the music, transcribed by Professor Torner, and the dance steps were deciphered independently of one another, it was found, when they were united, that they harmonised, even to the extent of the notes agreeing with certain of the individual steps.

THE GAVOTTE

" The sixth [*Bransle*] is called *La Gavot*, that is to say, the dance with song", writes Mersenne.

In the sixteenth century it was evidently a lively, springing dance, which stirred Arbeau to remark that "if this type of dance had been in fashion when my legs were young, I should not have failed to make notes of it". He explains that a *Gavotte* was "a collection of several *Bransles Doubles* which musicians have chosen and arranged in a sequence. . . . To this sequence they have given this name of *Gavotte*. They are danced in *duple* time with *petits sauts*. . . . But the dancers divide the *doubles* both *à droite* and *à gauche* by passages taken at will from the *Gaillardes*." The movements Arbeau suggests in his tabulation include springing and crossing steps, and a *capriole*.

Perhaps the reference to a "gaillarde trick of twentie", which occurs in Marston's *Brawle* in *The Malcontent* (1604), alluded to the *gaillarde* steps which were used in the *Gavotte*.

The *Gavottes* composed by the dancing-masters of the eighteenth century differed entirely from this original *Bransle*.

One of the tantalising blanks in the records of the dance has been caused by the notion, held by former historians of the art, that the *Gavotte* was far too well known to necessitate any description. The following extract, again from

DANCING

Mersenne, gives an indication of the dance, and of the manner in which the *Suite* ended.

"The *time* is *duple* [two-beat] and rather sedate. It forms the end of the *Bransles*, and, after it has been danced once or twice in the round, the person who had begun the *Bransle-à-Mener* makes a bow to his lady, before whom he dances only eight steps, and having taken her under his right arm, he makes her do a turn, and then do another on his left arm, each with eight steps. He then, having made a bow, takes her to her place and goes to his own. After each person has done the same thing in his turn, a general bow is made and each man takes his lady to the place whence he had taken her to dance."

Cotgrave's *Dictionary* (1611) describes a *Gavotte* as "a kind of Brawle, daunced commonly by one alone". This probably refers to the passage which each person danced in his turn, as quoted from Mersenne.

Mersenne calls the *Gavotte* "the dance with song". It is certain that singing was still a very usual accompaniment to dancing in the seventeenth century, as is seen by the collections of *Chansons pour danser* of this period.

From earliest times song has been the natural accompaniment of the dance, as it is still in numerous folk-dances in various parts of the world, the heritage of ages when many branches of culture, since grown apart, were considered, together with the life of the people, to be One.

BIBLIOGRAPHY OF BOOKS REFERRED TO IN THE INTRODUCTION AND NOTES

ARBEAU, THOINOT. *Orchésographie* (1588). (English translation by C. W. Beaumont. 1925.)
BOËHN, MAX VON. *Modes and Manners*, translated into English by Joan Joshua. (Harrap.)
CAROSO, FABRITIO. *Il Ballarino* (1581), and *Del Nobilta di Dame* (1603).
COURTIN, ANTOINE DE. *The Rules of Civility* (1671).
DAVIES, SIR JOHN. *Orchestra* (1596).
FEUILLET, RAOUL A. *Chorégraphie* (1701).
HAMBLY, W. D. *Tribal Dancing and Social Development* (1926). (Witherby.)
JENYNS, SOAME. *The Art of Dancing.* A poem (1728).
MERSENNE, MARIN. *Harmonie Universelle* (1636).
MURRAY, M. A. *The Witch-cult in Western Europe* (1921). (Clarendon Press.)
PEPYS, SAMUEL. *Diary* (1659–1665).
RAMEAU, P. *Le Maître à Danser* (1725). (English translation by C. W. Beaumont. 1931.)
RYE, W. B. *England as seen by Foreigners in the Days of Elizabeth and James I* (1865). (J. R. Smith.)
SHARP, C. J. *The Country Dance Book. Part 2* (1927). (Novello & Co.)
WALKER, NATHANIEL. *The Refined Courtier* (1663).
WEAVER, JOHN. *Orchesography* (1706).
WILLIAMSON, H. R. *George Villiers, 1st Duke of Buckingham* (1940). (Duckworth.)

METRICAL FEET USED IN THE *BRANSLES* AS GIVEN BY MARIN MERSENNE.

long—two syllables
short—one syllable

First Bransle	Dactyl : *long, short, short*	
	Spondee : *long, long*	
Second Bransle	Ionic : *short, short, long, long*	
Third Bransle	Fourth Peonique : *short, short, short, long*	
	First Peonique : *long, short, short, short*	
	Fourth Peonique : *short, short, short, long*	
Fourth Bransle	Iambic : *short, long*	
Fifth Bransle	Anapest : *short, short, long*	

INDEX

A

Académie Royale de la Danse, 18
Agrippa, 45
Allemande, 25, 55
Apollo, 61
Arabs, 170
Arbeau, Thoinot, 15, 16, 25, 28, 31, 32, 57, 166, 176, 179, 180, 186, 187, 188, 192, 193, 194, 197, 198, 199, 202, 203, 204, 206
Arena, Antoine, 55
Arion, 59
Aristarchus, 51
Aspasia, 61
Atheneus, 65

B

Ballet, 13, 17, 18, 25, 55, 196
Ballroom dancing, 14
Barre, 19
Bassedanse, 55
Bocan, 21, 22
Bocane, 22
Boëhn, 18
Bouffons, 55
Bow, 17, 24, 87, 91, 101, 119, 121, 162, 163, 164, 165, 166, 169, 171, 172, 174, 185
Brando, 29
Bransle, 14, 25, 26, 28, 29, 30, 31, 45, 55, 99, 101, 103, 105, 107, 109, 135, 136, 139, 141, 143, 147, 149, 179, 180, 193, 194, 196, 197, 198, 199, 216, 217
Brawl, 55, 217
Bretons, 55
Buckingham, see Villiers

C

Cadence, 89, 149, 186
Canaries, 25, 55
Caper, 177
Capriole, 89, 99, 113, 115, 176, 177, 178
Carole, 27, 28
Caroso, Fabritio, 176, 178, 188
Castanets, 32
Castlemaine, Lady, 29
Caus, Salomon de, 195
Celius, 65
Charles I, King, 20, 21
Charles II, King, 26, 29, 165
Chassé, 93, 95, 97, 111, 113, 147, 149, 182, 183, 191
Chassé coulant, 93, 182
Christian Church, 27, 61
Cicero, 65
Civility, Rules of, 24, 168, 171
Congy, 23
Contredanse, 55
Cordax, 55
Cordier, Jacques, 21
Costume, 15
Cotgrave, Dictionary, 217
Country-dance, 14, 31
Coupé, see Pas coupé
Courante, 14, 22, 25, 26, 30, 55, 87, 91, 95, 97, 99, 101, 139, 141, 145, 165, 171, 182, 191
Courtin, Antoine de, 23, 167, 168, 172
Curtsy, 17, 131, 133, 139, 171, 172, 173, 174, 175, 185

D

Damonides, 63
Dancing masters, 15, 21, 22, 23, 73, 75, 99, 109, 111, 113, 129, 147, 203, 212
Davies, Sir John, 26

INDEX

De Lauze, 15, 16, 17, 18, 25, 31, 32, 33, 162, 163, 165, 167, 174, 176, 178, 181, 182, 183, 186, 187, 188, 190, 191, 193, 197, 198, 199, 200, 202, 205, 210, 212, 215
Découpure, 135
Demi-capriole, 95, 99, 177, 178
Descartes, René, 16
Double, 179, 199
Double de Poitou, bransle, 141, 193, 197, 210

E

Education, dance-, 13, 22
Emelie, 55
English, 55, 168, 171
Entrechat, 177, 179
Entre-coupé, 99, 107, 181
Epaminondas, 65
Epimenides, 67

F

Feuillet, Raoul A., 177, 184
Five-steps, 113, 115, 149, 186, 187, 188, 189, 190
Flanders, 145
Fleuret, 99, 184
France, 55, 171

G

Galliard, 14, 30, 55, 87, 91, 111, 115, 149, 151, 177, 182, 185, 188, 189, 190, 191, 217
Gavotte, 31, 145, 193, 197, 216, 217
Gay, bransle, 105, 137, 193, 194, 196, 197, 202
Germans, 17, 55
Glissade, 143, 184, 211, 213, 215
Grove, Dictionary, 194, 196

H

Hambly, W. D., 176
Hat, wearing and taking off, 85, 91, 101, 119, 121, 162, 164, 165, 166, 171
Henrietta Maria, Queen, 22
Henry Frederick, Prince, 186

Homer, 63
Huberd, Lady Frances, 20

I

Italians, 55, 168, 170, 194

J

James I, King, 19, 20, 21
Jenyns, Soame, 33
Julius Polux, 65

K

Kiechel, Samuel, 168
King, 24, 26, 29, 31, 55, 69, 101, 164, 171, 172, 173
Kissing, 121, 165, 167, 168, 169, 170
Kissing of hands, 91, 101, 119, 121, 164, 165, 166, 167, 169, 170, 171, 204
Kneeling, 169

L

Louis XIV, King, 29
Lucian, 65
Lully, 194

M

Macrobe, 65
"Mal," Little, 20
Manners, 17, 166
Marston, John, 30, 205, 216
Masques, 17, 21
Master of Ceremony, 172
Mauritania, 55
Maypole dance, 29
Measures, 55, 192, 194
Medici, Marie de, 168
Mersenne, Marin, 16, 25, 31, 33, 189, 192, 193, 195, 196, 197, 198, 199, 200, 202, 203, 204, 206, 210, 212, 216, 217
Metassins, 55
Minuet, 13, 14, 15, 30, 173
Monmouth, Duke of, 29, 165, 170
Montague, 43, 47
Montirande, bransle de, 194, 197, 212
Moors, 55
More, Henry, 28

INDEX

Morisco, 55
Mouvemens, 195, 196, 197
Murray, M. A., 28
Music, 32, 155, 156, 157, 158, 159, 160, 161, 195, 215, 216

N

Nagas, 176
Netherlands, 168
Nicholas, Edward, 21
Normandy, 145
Normans, 55
Numa, 55

O

Orpheus, 59
Overture, 194

P

Pas assemblé, 105, 109, 139, 141, 143, 181, 182, 202, 207, 211
Pas chassé, 89
Pas couler, 183
Pas coupé, 99, 111, 143, 147, 149, 179, 180, 184, 190, 192, 206, 207, 209, 211, 212, 213, 214
Pas de courante, 89, 192
Pas de galliard, 187, 188
Pas glissé, 103, 105
Pas porté, 147, 191
Passemezzo, 25
Passepied, 55
Pavane, 25, 55
Pécour, Louis, 189, 205
Pembleton, 22, 23
Pepys, Samuel, 22, 23, 26, 29, 165, 169
Perrochie, 55
Petrie, Adam, 168
Pied-en-l'air, 179, 200, 202
Plato, 61, 63
Playford, John, 30
Plutarch, 63
Poitevins, 55
Poitou, bransle de, 31, 55, 105, 139, 183, 193, 196, 197, 203, 204, 210
Processional dance, 26, 27
Provence, 55
Puritans, 29

Q

Queen, 24, 26, 29, 31, 55, 172, 173

R

Rameau, P., 14, 15, 24, 25, 29, 31, 32, 163, 173, 184, 188, 192
Retirade, 93, 95, 97, 145, 185, 214
Rhythm, 32, 180, 194, 195, 197, (for the bransles) 200, 201, 202, 203, 204, 207, 208, 209, 211, 212, 213, 214, 215
Richelieu, Cardinal, 32
Ring dance, 28
Roscius, 65
Round dance, 26, 29, 31, 194
Rye, W. B., 168, 186

S

Sarabande, 25, 31, 32
Saracens, 31
Salii, 55
Scaliger, 55, 65
Scottish, 55
Seneca, 67
Sharp, Cecil, 30
Siccenix, 55
Simple, bransle, 135, 193, 194, 197, 198, 199
Singles (simples), 179
Siris, P., 177
Socrates, 61, 63
Sophia, Electress, of Hanover, 17
Spaniards, 55, 168
Stoics, 59
Suite of bransles, 32, 99, 109, 143, 192, 193, 197

T

Temps en rond, 93, 95
"Tom Duff," 20
Tordion, 55
Torner, E. M., 200, 216
Tradition, 13
Triory, 55
"Turn out," of the legs, 18, 85, 101, 113, 129, 131, 135
Twelfth Night, 177

INDEX

V

Villiers, George, 1st Duke of Buckingham, 19, 20, 21, 37, 45
Villiers, Katherine, 20, 127
Villiers, Mary, 20, 32
Volta, 25, 55

W

Walker, Nathaniel, 170
Walking, 85, 131
Waterman, George, 23

Weaver, John, 14, 177
Williamson, H. R., 19, 21
Wirtschaft, 17

X

Xenophon, 65

Y

York, Duchess of, 29
York, Duke of, 26, 29

www.ingramcontent.com/pod-product-compliance
Lightning Source LLC
Chambersburg PA
CBHW070041230426
43661CB00027B/1321